MARKETS & THE LIABILITY
OF AMERICAN BUSINESS

MARKETS & THE LIABILITY OF AMERICAN BUSINESS 2011 MARKETS IN THE UNITED STATES AND TODAYS ECONOMY & GOVERNMENT

iUniverse books may be ordered through booksellers or by contacting:

iUniverse
1663 Liberty Drive
Bloomington, IN 47403
www.iuniverse.com
1-800-Authors (1-800-288-4677)

Because of the dynamic nature of the Internet, any web addresses or links contained in this book may have changed since publication and may no longer be valid. The views expressed in this work are solely those of the author and do not necessarily reflect the views of the publisher, and the publisher hereby disclaims any responsibility for them.

Any people depicted in stock imagery provided by Thinkstock are models, and such images are being used for illustrative purposes only.

Certain stock imagery © Thinkstock.

ISBN: 978-1-4620-0123-1 (sc)
ISBN: 978-1-4620-0124-8 (e)

Printed in the United States of America

iUniverse rev. date: 06/09/2011

MARKETS &
THE LIABILITY OF
AMERICAN
BUSINESS

2011 MARKETS
IN THE UNITED STATES
AND TODAY'S ECONOMY
& GOVERNMENT

JAYSON REEVES

iUniverse, Inc.
Bloomington

INTRODUCTION

Understanding and observing, the markets and liability of American businesses over the last 50 to 100 years up to the millennium years of the 2000s has consisted of many changes. These market and business conflicts including considerable issues were valued to establish safe, lawful, productive, and efficient products, and services. This becomes a vital duty, and subject within most diversified business operations consisting of the concern that some products or services may not perform right or the best with liability the first time. Our American society of businesses, have understood this foundation of liability most time to eliminate an enormous amount of problems. Lately, during the decades of the 1990s, and 2000s certain factual problems have range from bankruptcy, credit delinquencies, prime lending conflicts, fatal plant explosions, and other things that may require better government, and business employee involvement. In addition this effort may become a vital concern in the American system of court's, and most levels, and branches of government.

Over the years of 1990, to 2005 economic liquidity problems and issues have included sub-prime lending, prime lending, non-traditional lending, and other factual issues of business transactions consisting of market matters within a financial "Junk Bond" market that is out of control. Observing the United States financial markets with corporate businesses that were established in America with investments, certain junk-bond and "merger" activity has allowed foreign business people to take control of too many American markets, and corporations. These factors have eliminated billions, and trillions of dollars of economic interest from a vast amount of commodities that American's depend on. Then, this American format of a money circulation is a vital issue to observe. Upon various events this book will explain these subjects of business liabilities within small, large, public, and private businesses. These business factors include the liabilities of economic liquidity that is applicable for the requirements of most all levels, and individual state governments, including the United States federal government, and how it applies to all other American's, and businesses. Therefore the liability of liquidity within American markets is to be determined from productive business, and American people without anti-competitive conflicts of deception.

Observing good, and bad mergers, hostile takeovers, and companies that are financially considered junk-bond rated, it takes time to see the results. This issue has lost liability with anti-competitive values within opportunities to maintain solid growth within liquidity. Within the levels of concerned understanding the people must value that liability is one of our most important issues of "significant responsibility". This significant responsibility is also a duty considering that this appropriates the people, businesses, and government powers of lawfully authentic disciplines of identity. All markets, and issues of business with personal liability in our American society go thru these changing times, and factors with complications to with complications. This exist to secure liquidity in business transactions, merger's, and buyout's with government, and or the lawful resources of affirmations. Upon these good, and bad factors during this time (c/o the 1st decade of 2000) within markets, each corrected or restructured business value has occasionally enhanced these issues that have critical nerve conditions applied to liquidation or liquidity.

This book will also outline some of the major and minor issues of markets in the United States that the people of the public and even government including certain businesses, and corporations depend on respectfully. Within these formal issues of business, and markets an even more important fact is the relevant duty of the govern judiciary of the states, and the United States federal government to keep court room negligence, and judicial conduct in order for the markets, and the people. This goes along with keeping professional negligence and crime of all kinds at a low rate. Apart from markets, and professional issues of liability some court proceeding's like some other things during the 1990s has factored high levels of negligence. Occupational and professional conflicting issues to be enforced lawfully by the courts in a timely matter as it relates to business and even national security occasionally became disastrous. Therefore this makes the American court system important for lawful business, and the American society of people whom on occasions have a need for justice to be served, or destructive acts prevented.

Most all markets, and sectors of American business that are valued in the oil industry, the automobile industry, the steel industry, retail clothing and food industries, and the markets of different commodity's including the format of agriculture products where established for survival, and earning money. Considering this, these different market issues, and conditions consist of more so the good of American values. It becomes relevant also in the professions of internal medicine, agriculture, law, engineering, and architecture that applies to construction, manufacturing, and or healthcare which also consist of "liability facts, and the U.S. Anti-Trust laws" to balance most competitive, and lawful differences.

The American society, and the United States government provides U.S. Anti-Trust laws, and the United States Constitution with the format of the executive, legislative, and judicial branches of government to oversee these issues of liability that are relevant in most all diversified business markets. This is a vital part of the Separation of Powers that no branch of the American government is more powerful than the other, just like the fair market competitive resources of business. Within format of various United States government regulation, and the observation of markets with liabilities, this is factored for the concern that some of these laws, and regulation go back within time of nearly one hundred years, or more. Also within the same concept of duties, and responsibilities there has been factors of governed negligence, and success that is occasionally pondered with failure. Education and hard work that includes the understanding of how certain parts of government work, and the right people for the right subjects or positions is also a vital part of eliminating certain conditions of failure. This also includes the American publicly traded companies in the Securities and Exchange markets of the United States, within Americas different region's considering "new, and old" business issues.

The term liability throughout our American society is highly used, and considered by most to all insurance companies, as well banks, investment banking establishments, and other industries. Considering this, the format of other markets, within business observe this as a significant duty within legal responsibility. The writing, and reading of this book (Markets & The Liability of American Business) the Author, Jayson Reeves will discuss our past, and present business factors of concern, and social conditions of business, banking, investment banking, and some insurance company's. These conditions of society within business, and corporations is part of the people obligation throughout industry. This becomes issues in the American society that excepts, applies, and considers the facts of how productive factual issues have been observed to appropriate valued concern to the American society. Besides the lack of governed liability, and damage's on September 11, 2001, American's also suffered with the 2005 Hurricane Katrina that included other natural disasters where people, and assets suffered severely. Also throughout the United States, corporations in the manufacturing of steel products, and other product industry's has suffered with expensive levels of damage from fatal explosions. Lack of discipline considering negligence became a complacent problem causing some of these fatal explosions, or accidents. This is the consideration that factually all of these issues of accidents have liability concerns that effect a diversified consideration of people, and markets. Along with the former Enron Corporation, these have been American business issues with good, and sometimes vitally bad "market and work place liability" issues, including conflicts within "market, and business" liquidity.

Understanding issues, and legal disciplines that apply to the U.S. Anti-Trust laws, and more so the significance of liabilities in American businesses, these factual issues will be reviewed with observation of certain company's like the Ford Motor Company, WorldCom Corporations, American Telephone & Telegraph Corporation, and the Enron Corporation. Also this is applicable to some television, radio, and newspaper market businesses, and their format of the changing times of productive American business with government. Most of these changing times have applicable duties, and responsibilities within certain corporations that include National Broadcasting Corporation (NBC), and American Broadcasting Corporation (ABC) with the good, and bad of internet excessive activities. Some other issues (c/o Microsoft Corp & National Broadcasting Corp {MSNBC}) during today consist of the discretionary good and bad of the "World Wide Web" Internet systems of our life as it applies today with the format of certain markets. It would seem that so many different advances in our American society, and certain regional economic factors, and resources would be improving, but it is important to remember that the state and federal government system of our American society only slightly recognized these liability issues including international investments that seem to bring international terrorism.

Considering the laws, and certain markets this is the problem were the courts, and more so the legislative branch have failed to stay ahead of good, and more so bad technology that has hurt certain markets, businesses, and people. This means that upon all public, private business, and government, America did not prevent certain conflicting problems. These factors vitally include illegal immigration, defamation of character, destructive business transactions, and other discretionary subjects including terrorism. Therefore the good, and bad of the people have transformed our American economy too support people's access from other foreign borders more so then "the vital access, and support of certain important or valued American citizens".

The objective of good and bad foreign relations observing our United States government, and how the laws are enforced considering "international investments, and international terror", has become a complicated deterrent for most business markets, and all American born citizens. Also, included in these issues of crime and terrorist activities which occasionally has been supported by certain American born citizens, this was the radical views to obstruct progress in the United States. American corporations and the concern of the citizens of the general public, including all levels of government in America must take these issues serious. Observing the format of market's the U.S. Anti-Trust laws, most liabilities, and the U.S. Securities and Exchange rules and laws are applicable to most citizenship values for the concept within these corporate American duties.

It's vital to observe these issued subjects to the good, and bad of "foreign and American" relations which, includes U.S. National Security decisions, and some business and government concerns. This has potential to threaten our American society, and these fair values within the important ways we find liable agreements, disagreements, and then must guild these concerns in the right direction, and not the wrong direction, and ways. The people, and citizens of America from time to time already must dispute certain factors of business, social issues, corporate conflicts in the courts, and even government occasionally when we become victimized by the highs, and lows of corporate management, and even labor organizations. This includes also the good, and more so bad products, and services of our American society whether in, or out of the courts. This has been observed over the last couple centuries with the good, bad, and applicable disputes for what the United States Constitution prescribes within our government's agenda. These issues of a well "developed" American society, and governed agenda is the foundation for all people considering (for the people & by the people) being the importance of working together to establish a balanced, and disciplined American society. Therefore the markets, liabilities, and businesses that include the people, has potential for the best solutions possible in America.

Table of Contents

How Markets Where Established In America
(1)

CHAPTER ONE
(1)

The United States Library of Congress

How Markets Where Established In America
(1)

The diversified markets in America where established over the hundreds of years that the people have worked with public, private businesses, and government factors throughout the United States, and the American territories. Most businesses long ago from the 1880s to the 1970s, 80s, and 90s have accumulated a commitment with the most important values of the changing times within American marketable products, services, and even the duties of government. This also includes the many ways money, and other legal tender values such as gold, and silver has been discovered, and produced to maintain market, and currency value. A person can also observe these market values of monetary conditions for these different metals, and even their values within precious metal conditions as part of an established market. Many other steel, and sheet metal by-products are used for thousands of other products for its level of material load capacity strengths. Therefore metals (c/o limestone and ore), wood from trees, including so many other commodities similar to coal, wheat, or corn are just a few products with a wide range of markets throughout America, and other places.

Precious metals including currency issues in our American society have become important to considerably all diversified market's, the people, and government within issues of financial leverage which is relevant for the valid use of those materials. This observation applies to silver, copper, and especially gold as it applies to the rate of currency upon which at certain times is part of a valid monetary indicated standard. Other different metals provide products such as metal (musket ball) bullets, copper bullets, and certain piping. Also metal water pipes within well equipment, most all water pumps, building components and years later certain sewer drainage equipment with most vehicle wheel, and mechanical components have become vital metal materials that are used, and that becomes helpful to the American society.

Precious metals within gold, silver, and copper are factored within the consolidated format of jewelry, and certain legal coins of money. This metal is part of the rate of coins that goes into production, and circulation every year throughout the United States which is applied to the currency markets. In addition metals are important for various housing, and building components that also includes parts of a barn with the storage of some animals in mind, and this includes housing components providing people with public health values. From this observation, products, and assets that have a value, and currency market upon the consideration of the United States Mint (sense 1652 & 1792), are within the American resources of assets, and governed management that have been around for a long time. These concerns are within the changes that will continue to arrange the American businesses, government, and the general public.

Everything from the resource of marketable products such as boats, horses, cattle, oil, land, and even covered carriage wagons; "American products, and markets where becoming diversified" throughout the decade of the 1880's, and up to the 1990's. This observation would include the important values within the expanding products within the American automobile industry. These markets would be consistent of the responsibilities between merchants, and customers to pay, receive, and carry. Even guns were made, and marketed for protection, and hunting. Also oil became a commodity just like the various amounts of agriculture farming products, and farming tools to keep soil, crops, and livestock farming productive. Agriculture and farming has been a food growing, and farm animal livestock process for century's in the United States with issues that have factored good, and some bad changes within certain observed productive outcomes. All of these products, and other things within large, and small volume's or capacities where part of some form of marketing with a money, and currency circulation. Therefore the format of taxable earnings with economic issues apply to all, just as the services that are provided by bank establishments for people, and businesses dating back from the 1880's to now during the years of 2000.

Considering the business, and marketing of banking products, and services the American banking system has changed, but it still consist of transactions, liabilities for their clients bank deposits, withdraws, and other money accounts that may format business, auto, and home lending. These things are based on the offered provisions within the bank services that they are providing discipline with concerns to some reliable details of negotiated standards. Over the last 70 years (c/o the 1930's) the Federal Deposit Insurance Corporation was established to format levels of security for the depositors of the bank, and this is "Backed By The Full Faith Credit Of The United States Congress, and Government". The commerce bank format and the concept of investment banking have went through many changes sense then, and therefore during 2010 the issue of liability must be revised with certain details all over again.

The difference between the Enron Corporation's financial failure and collapse, and the Great Depression of the 1920's & 1930's is that the corporation is responsible for its own accounting, and business issues of liability which includes the good, and bad of new technology. This was a company that also tried to establish a market, and it failed as an "energy trading company"! The American format and resource of regulating the markets of "Energy" (c/o the U.S. Department of

Energy) was formally established in the United States during 1977 in the President Jimmy Carter Administration. When we compare American banking to energy as it applies to public utilities, and "holding company's" the format of banking goes back a bit further with strict disciplines as well because these are broad markets to the general public with important liability concerns. These markets have changed over the decades with regulation, and corporate disciplines due to the valued earnings, and some monopoly, and holding company disciplines of liquidity that appropriate resourceful markets throughout the American society.

The state and federal bank system including local or commerce banking have levels of bank fund managing, and accounting responsibilities with lawful support from the United States Federal Reserve Bank system. This provides discount lending, and security measures of liquidity for all small, large, and diversified accounts that are managed under the bank, or business format of the management, and the American system of government. The Great Depression was a business stock trading disaster upon where corporations and government had not established a legal regulatory discipline to secure the economic issues of the changing times.

During the 1920's the people lost in various different ways, and now up to the 1990s, and 2000's we have learned a lesson about liabilities, manageable liquidity, and security, but other facts of awareness exist such as over-sight technology. The concept of over-sight technology with new advances have given people a good way of doing things faster with information technology, but they can also commit vary serious crimes (c/o finance & violence) as well, therefore our system of government legislature must keep up.

Observing 33 years before the 1929 Great Depression in 1897 a man named Charles Dow a financial publisher (c/o his firm) calculated a financial stock average that consisted of a market of 12 company's trading in America. Years later with marketable investments providing market and business growth, the Dow Jones Averages was established to consist of: (one) an average of the common stock prices of 30 industrial firms, (two) an average of common stock prices of 20 transportation companies, (three) an average of common stock prices of 15 utility companies, and (four) an average of 65 stock prices. This became the market divisor calculated process of maintaining a day, by day opening and closing price of the stock market, currency, and even commodity exchange's. Considering a majority of these diversified companies, and firms they had grown within numbers of corporate offices, industrial plants, and special types of businesses. The major stock exchanges are now managed by their establishments within people as board of directors, staff members, and regional facilities. In addition they are part of the decision making process for a company that may want to be offered as an investment entity that is actively traded within certain exchange markets. Observing this format of marketable investments, this is, and was established upon all the good, and bad that may exist within the resources of the American society, and business issues of a compounded economic discipline that possibly can advance financially.

The financial advances, and losses by the American investors, and people concerning the liabilities of banks, businesses, and corporations has been diversified approaching the 1990s, and these recent years which have outlined most of these values of prosperity. These different business liabilities within the outlined examples of the Great Depression being the worse, was because during 1929 thousands (1000s) of banks closed along with a vast amount of businesses. Enormous amounts of people, and corporate stock shareholders lost all their investments in the stock market crash with some other people penniless because of businesses that where closing, and the loss of jobs. Sense those years of the 1930s, and the 1940s the United States government and the people pulled together with programs to help the needy, and those that were prepared, and able to work. The effects that banking and investing has own most individual American's, and businesses can, and has been tremendous with lawfully important future issues to understand.

The decade after 1920, and 1930 during the U.S. Presidency's of Hubert Hoover, and Franklin D. Roosevelt consisted of good and bad issues of satisfaction about the American system of government. This included factors of how to solve the problems of a complex market, and economy within business during that period of an economic depression. Observing 1995 and 2000, the largest concept of liability, and depressed economic business factors has been the Enron Corporation, the WorldCom Corporation, the arbitration of certain internet companies, the Ford Motor Company, and lately a variation of banking establishments. The corporate, and government failures of the 1990s, and 2000 did not affect as many people as of yet, but more companies have been added to this list of a financial crisis, and it could become even more devastating.

During the 1990's the loss of Montgomery Ward's with dept. stores, Service Merchandise Corp with dept. stores, Zayer's Corp. with dept. stores, and a few others caused a large loss of market share in certain retail store markets. This also caused a lack of opportunities of employment which included a forfeiture percentage of government tax revenue. This means everyone loses something! The numbers within financial losses for various businesses exceeds $50,000,000,000.00 (billion) dollars easily, and some mortgage lenders, and bank's including investment bank's whom are starting to consolidate the same, may go into the losses of "trillions"of dollars.

If we look at the market concerned activities of good and bad in the oil industry, the steel industry, investment banking, and various markets upon how it includes mortgage lending banks today, there are some interesting, but critical worries. This concern even more so, includes the multiple-sided issues within household economics, and some national security issues of international business in America. This format of interesting worries consist of the difference that before, and during the 1960s, and 1970s American people (c/o a person or couple) could pay for a house within 30 years. Now during the 1990s, and the years of 2000 a vast amount of people are lucky if they can pay, and survive in a house for 10 years. This is the partial result of unemployment, some international out-sourcing of jobs, and managing issues including some bad adjustable mortgage issues within bank interest rates.

Another economic and industry concern includes some bank lending requirements that change with unproductive business decisions. Besides banking the people, and various businesses have recognized problems that include tax concerns with rapid conflicts. Sometimes these factors are similar to the banks that make mistakes that can't be corrected easily, and then they are occasionally managed with hopes not to threaten the wealth or other deposits throughout the business resources within other commitments. Other factual problems can occur when the older Americans get strapped with complex bills, and therefore they may require certain help from the youthful members of their family if appropriate. With too many young people concerned about crime (apart from gainful employment and guidance), this becomes a rare condition of security for some elderly, and even others like infant children, but some people are adjusting with the times.

A formal consideration is that, there have been occasions with the automobile, and steel industry lay-offs or employee buyouts that occur due to business market slowdowns that have caused people to suffer, or reorganize within their homes, and different assets. Various amounts of people sometime don't manage these employee buyout funds like others. This especially is considerate when the American system of stock market, and commodity exchanges consist of troubling factors, and therefore a percentage of problems may occur from these terminal decisions about investing for the future. Within these factors it is relevant that all businesses and banking work together with productive social values for citizens in a productive capacity. Throughout all good and bad changing times, this therefore includes the awareness of manipulation or any conflicts that won't mislead the general public as consumers, and occasionally as long-term investors.

Considering the large capacity of bank mergers whether small or large they consist of certain issues from these business transactions that have destroyed the sacrifices, and payment planning of various citizens, and business owners. This is more to be considered within the format of job security, and bank lending agreements including even the complexity of the new ownership within management. This is the economic liability format that most local banks have maintained from serving customers with savings, and checking account stability. Also these bank businesses are considered as being a trust worthy bank within lending, and managing small and large accounts of money. Observing this also includes the money, and investment assets that employees, and bank board members put back into the banking establishment for their own retirement, and financial security. Having, and understanding this form of banking, and business transactions including investment banks also requires the liability laws of "Privacy Rights, and Confidentiality". Upon the fact of confidentiality with logical disciplines of affirmation these one or two problems are maintained within a diversified concentration of stable decisions within personal, and business establishments.

With the format, and laws understanding "Privacy Rights and Confidentiality" (upon Affirmations) the United States has consisted of some of the worse levels of "Constitutional Law" enforcement, and compliance (c/o the 1990s to 2011) than most times in the history of America. It has become almost as bad as Adolph Hitler invading the privacy rights of people in Germany, and then killing them with one large hole for a burial. Considering this day, and time of "Confidentiality and Privacy Rights" violations against the American people, and some small businesses, their efforts are being put in a large hole of financial debt with very little life expectations. Observing this, it is important to remember that doors, walls, and even windows where invented during, and after houses to let people come in, go out, and most times this restricted anything, or anybody not to be let in. Telephone systems are similar, considering what you want communicated to other people and even what you don't' occasionally want to talk or communicate to others about. The United States Federal Privacy Act forbids these types of violations, and problems that occasionally involved a person's confidential equity, liabilities, mental solitude, domestic tranquility, and other issues which, dates back nearly one hundred years. This also becomes true in small and large businesses upon them having provisions of "affirmation and conformation" duties within their day by day transactions, business planning, and various responsibilities.

It is vital for a person, or business to take the liability within privacy rights, and normal confidentiality serious. This state and federal right of privacy for most all people in American cities, and towns keep the mental, and moral solitude of relations, and diversified business concerns in complete order especially as it applies to the people's planed sacrifices. When these factual issues, and laws are ignored and deprived just as a judge is to comply, and enforce the state, and U.S. federal Constitutions of our American society businesses, markets, and the people suffer. This vitally includes how they are subjected to living within a lack of full sovereignty, and despair. This means our prosperity, and sometimes our domestic tranquility has been severely threatened.

My observation with a few others can be considered from the market events, and activities of the former Ameritech Corporation that was a disaster compared to the formal establishment of the

Bell Telephone Systems, and Laboratories. The American telephone and communications markets where established by the inventions of Alexander Bell with help from Thomas Edison (c/o his discovery of electricity) during the 1870s that started the Bell Company. Years later the Federal Communications Commission (FCC) was added by the United States government to regulate the expanding, and massive American television, and radio market's which also includes different communication systems, and telephone systems with various equipment. The design of the telephone looked procurer up until the 1930s, and at that time numbers were added to identify other telephone connections. These types of changes will continue into the future with the need of laws that keep the American society disciplined.

Ameritech during the 1990s lacked certain lawful duties within the United States Constitutional disciplines of a well-established, and moral society which where activities pursued with unprofessional objectives in other lawful business concerns, and agreements that could not be ignored. The Ameritech Corporation had some good, but just like Enron Corporation, Ameritech Corporation lacked enormous professional codes of conduct, and ethics that occasionally included the exploitation of woman sexually, or woman that wanted to be exploited thru television communication affairs. This sad liability, and marketing problem (c/o the FCC) was incorporated between television companies, and the phone company's upon which they seemed to want to sale sex more then be a lawfully ethical, and productive telephone (advertising) service company. It also seems that Ameritech Corporation, and WorldCom Corporation had problems respecting certain U.S. Anti-Trust legal rights of other businesses that included the 1st & 4th Amendments of the United States Constitution. As this went "on and on" without judicial review, or the prosecution of FCC indecency, and solicitation rules, and laws considered, the United States Department of Justice allowed marriage, small businesses, and citizens to severely suffer. This went on without proper interruption, and lawful corrections before problems increased.

Understanding the businesses, and markets of Ameritech and WorldCom it strongly seem as thou some of their activities on too many occasions victimized people, and other businesses that consolidated a need for legal compensation or victim relief. Observing these matters certain businesses and some government officials became a negative issue of concern within the format of U.S. National Security violations that took advantage of innocent hardworking Americans, and then supported people from enemy countries.

Chicago is one of the few large cities where occasionally various national security conflicts occur with matters from people like William Daly whom resigned from Ameritech, and then went to work at the U.S. Department of Commerce. He helped an eroding process of social values get worse, and with other conflicts throughout the American society of businesses which was hit "worse, and worse" which certain regions and businesses suffered tremendously! Some say the WorldCom Corporation with Bernard Ebbers was even worse as it applies to U.S. Anti-Trust law violations, but the combination of continued bad businesses pushed the U.S. Economy into a destructive direction. Considering the format of progress within also being government contractors (c/o Ameritech) these are bad factors including how these corporations (c/o even the U.S. government) did not help prevent the September 11, 2001 attacks. Therefore we as Americans hope all lessons, and government disciplines will be adjusted lawfully, and accordingly, especially at the rate of new, and or certain American markets that are not lawfully or completely workable with liability!

Another lesson of government liabilities that occasionally includes markets in what American's have suffered from with Hurricane Katrina in New Orleans, Louisiana and certain parts of

Mississippi has created added worries that needed to be corrected. The consideration of government, and businesses have known about this problem of hurricanes in the Gulf Coast states way before our American society ever built dams, and the levees that worked, or failed. This flood problem killed (over 1,500) people, and destroyed a vast amount of business assets, and residential properties in 2005 during the month of August. Insurance companies and various businesses found themselves in a contingent liability disaster. Contrary to these subjects this regional consolidated market (c/o seafood and oil) became the U.S. government concern to help reorganize the hardest hit parts of the city of New Orleans. This vitally includes the vast amount of federal government funds that will be committed to this Gulf Coast region.

These Gulf Coast types of federal government (Emergency) funded projects is part of a serious marketing concern, and more so in conjunction with the Executive Order's (c/o President George Bush) providing factors of the disaster. All issues within the massive disaster that occurred within our American decelerated format of liability is slightly unfulfilled with corrections that factored this serious problem. These factors of disaster and the American system of government including even public utility companies have had to maintain these cost concerns (feasibility-analyses) that are done to access all damage. The relevance of this becomes part of their marketing strategy for sub-contractors to increase the liability of services for these regional customers, and the people that they serve.

Public utilities and government from time to time work in various different markets with new, old, but importantly vital industry concerns. Professionals of engineering, and the issued sense of events before construction of the Hoover Dam, the Brooklyn Bridge, the Golden Gate Bridge, and 1000s of smaller dam's, roadway's, highway's, levee's, and even nuclear plants were considered vital markets of improving certain values of the American infrastructure. These scientific engineering projects made public safety better for American's, and this became a productive resource for earning wages. These were part of the expanding resources of infrastructures including the construction that developed America's society of supportive public, private utility systems, and comparable government structures. Government owned utilities, and the public, or private owned utilities are incorporated in these "resources upon emanate domain" monopolized issues that serve the American society with professionals of scientific duties, and liability. Working properly together this provides safety, and levels of efficiency when all people from different American cities, towns, and other regions have access from most utility-infrastructure concerns of logical service usage. This from time to time is part of what people consider as our well-developed American society, but these infrastructures with industrial processes require maintenance. This regular maintenance (c/o lack of efficiency) within American infrastructures is the vital responsibility of the city, town, state, county, and the U.S. federal government's commitment of duty upon which includes some business liability concerns.

The businesses that maintain high levels of quality, and liability without too much excessive cost are the businesses that achieve good ratings, and then expand. Most times they suffer less problem's, from employees, and customers, and this usually requires good managing skills. Within diverse factors, most of these considered good, and bad issues of business quality values, including liabilities, the United States Anti-Trust laws are even more vital in helping expansion minded business owners. Considering this the business owners work more effective with others too consider better values of how to maintain or expand their business awareness within prosperous logic. A small and productive business needs these regulatory facts of law when larger competitors and others will from time to time instigate, or manipulate their sacrifices of business. Then small and large businesses, corporations, and especially business owners (c/o leadership) must take observation of disclosers, and the Federal Privacy Act to keep their market share, and or cliental lawfully satisfied. This is also valuable to appropriate the consolidated business issues that are good, and bad for the business with the best decisions possible.

Some of the major oil, and steel company's upon industry management have did things wrong in both directions considering labor, and against smaller businesses such as food, and gas station franchise's. This has been factored from legal maneuvers that start with defamation of American workers, to promote foreign workers. In large, certain corporate manufactures which included some employees working for less than a year, and then the management would fire them, or cause trouble to the employee before they join the union, or advance into upper management, became an American tragedy. The union has some good causes which "intervenes" with some occasional bad decisions. Another conflict is the defamation of a franchise business owner that may suffer some conflicts of manipulation, and privacy rights violations especially as it occurred in 1991. Some corporations have taken themselves into a financial hole of trouble with these tactics. Then from all of these conflicting subjects, most industry factors go back to the banking responsibilities of understanding the businesses. Considering most of these industry concerns are market evaluated decisions with other issues that are a formal concern, then the process becomes a needed condition of review. In addition these resources must be formatted lawfully for the long-term factor of business including job security issues that become vitally important as an overall social discipline in Americas future.

If the consideration of the executive, legislative, and judicial branches of the American system of government accepts the best decisions for the right conditions, our American society will benefit from enforceable laws with valued court proceeding, and government without negative conflicts of interest. This also means that any solutions of lawful prosperity with most of our American markets, and issues of liability will factor progress. This progress will be for the good, or bad of established procedures to improve within most good markets. Then this is the format of business, and government long-term progress that makes businesses aware that government is doing their part along with the American people, and markets. Without this formal condition, and concept of issues, most priorities within government have an observation of thousands or more businesses, and households suffering financially. These households and businesses are suffering financially from a damage infested real estate / mortgage market, and economy with high rates of property foreclosure's. Contrary to the fact during 2009, and 2010 some undamaged, or new housing developments are suffering as well. This is the near break of what some professionals observe as a near (social & economic) depression, or recession leveled concept of problems. Our American society can do better, but this takes disciplines of business, and government planning within certain conditions of a workable format. Then the lawful American society, that we live in can more so work together proving effort, and proper solutions within all components of a well developed lively hood.

A format within years of development, and market's consist of ratings that the United States Department of Commerce keeps track, and measure of is the United States "Gross National Production" (GNP) rate. The Gross Domestic Product (GDP) rate is observed just as important, considering it applies to the American disciplines of public, private industries, and businesses. Observing the United States gross national product this consist of the entire value of goods, and services produced, marketed, and considerably sold in America. This economic indication of measurements consist of small, and large businesses including corporations considering any whole sale, and distribution process of products manufactured, and sold as lawful item's (with some internationally) in the United States.

Considering the U.S. GNP rate system in the start of the 1900's was around $18.7 billion dollars, worth of product items, this mostly came from American businesses. This rate increased in products and sales by the 1970s to $1.075 trillion dollars with issues of inflation, and accumulated value which had more foreign products included. Observing 2008 the GNP is $14.7 trillion dollars, and the GDP is $14.59 trillion dollars which is sometimes affected by deficit matters. These factors become the consolidation of a massive amount of products that were manufactured, developed, and most all the products even tested, and sold. Most American people or professionals including some foreign people, and certain U.S. government officials observed this diversified consolidation of products with occasional liabilities as factually good. In some concerns it takes a million or more dollars to track, keep up with, and possibly live thru the understood evaluation of these numbers annually or within a decade. Therefore it might be logical to leave it as the United States Department of Commerce's duty, and a lone few professional souls. A better observation is that this is what a tax base is factored from including the workers to pay government taxes, upon which provides a U.S. Constitutional society of revenue shearing, and discipline.

Within these major, and minor priced items of our American society we will find durable goods such as automobiles, computers, most all houses, televisions, appliances, and other products compounded with different coordinated materials. Then we have an understanding of non-durable goods such as foods, utilities, and services such as barber's, beautician's, hospital and healthcare concerns. Also some factors of entertainment within the relevant concept of reliable gross domestic product levels within marketable resources exist in other conditional markets as well. A more simple consideration besides most large capacity economist; is that the smallest items in cost or size, to the highest cost within sized items, is an accountable tax generating capacity of money. Clearly the general public, most times have appreciation of these purchases that businesses are offering within these different products, and services within marketing from the business's with a concept of liability.

Now, there is a valued understanding of products, markets, and liabilities that the people provide (c/o some business) in the many different regions of America. Most times the United States of America, and it's geological regional commodities can sometimes be understood for the certain products, and levels of employment which is supported by earnings that appropriates a region's economy. This is where people, management and the good, and bad of labor unions (c/o some nonunion businesses), and not to many others observing the consumers upon working together try to make a company's products, and or services the best. An array of products, or commodities usually consist of oil, coal, livestock animals, food crops, and various agriculture by-products. In appropriate addition this also consist of different specified components from the lakes, rivers, and oceans like sea food, and a vast amount of other marketable items of concern. From the east coast, the west coast, and the north, and south the diversified resource of markets, and goods is applicable to American prosperity, and the welfare conditional values of nature, and the geological society. Understanding this, it's important not to forget the commitment of most levels of government within cities, towns, states, and the federal government to provide value to their logical tax base. All these established markets are helpful, and are logical components of working together that are within the solutions for our well-developed American society. Therefore this process of the American developed society offer it's best products, and services with advancements, and prosperity for all market's, businesses, and or citizens.

The American System Of Liabilities & Business
(2)

CHAPTER TWO
(2)

The United States Library of Congress

The American System Of Liabilities & Business (2)

Within the American system of liabilities, and business the United States has established some good issues of formal products, and services with certain attempts to change things that may not work as good for the people, and society. During the United States Presidential tenor of Bill Clinton: him, and some of his constituents wanted to support the development of a computer system where people could sign documents on a computer to transmit a copy to certain lawful data base locations, and or relevant places of business. This was an attempt for something that occasionally consisted of bad issues of concerned liability from government for most all parts of our American society, but it did have some workable components. In logical reference, no form of responsible technology in the United States was made, developed, or established to commit crimes, but it is vital within issues of liability, and oversight to understand that it can happen. Actually with some rates of domestic violence, and financial crimes which includes new technology, this has occasionally been an instigated threat to liability. Therefore "caution", and future legislature is relevant!

Observing the rate of "business, and personal economic failures" during 2002 thru 2009 with oversights of technology (c/o negligence & crime) has cost people, government, and businesses small fortunes of money that add up. Due to this fact of when liability problems occur, business resource activities, and certain contractual damages of unfulfilled work could increase, and the victims, and government sometimes haven't responded fast enough with some of the best technology. The largest businesses (c/o some wealthy people) occasionally survive better with adjustable values of asset liquidity, if they are not part of crime, and negligent conflicts.

Most small businesses around the United States that are just starting to do business productively at certain profitable levels cannot afford certain unnecessary expenses, and damage "over and over" again. This may be the reason why new business openings have slowed down over the years. A consistent flow of bad expenses eliminates what earnings, and financial profit's a new business is starting to make with liability. Even the expenses of taking other people, or businesses to court becomes delicate with ethical standards, but sometimes this is aggressively vital, and important with disciplines upon factual cost. A comparison is observed when American citizens that where in a mad rush seeking government help from bank foreclosures (c/o 2008 to 2010) left people idol which means they had to put more trust in government than normal for any solutions.

The consideration of cost, and liability go "hand, and hand" consistently with making the best business, and social decisions possible. Any and most all businesses of America most times understand the liability within the first few months, and years of a new business are some of the most critical, respectfully, and financially! This observation implies that the best business decisions will more so provide the best business outcome. These decisions, and solutions will sometimes consist of having the best people for the money, and then them providing responsible duties. The small business owner is very different from some large business owners (c/o certain similarities) that are very different within equity, and cash conditions to operate the business. Considering this, some large business start up's consisted of where there may be an outrageous amount of cash on hand with more responsibilities. These types of businesses consist of the small, and or large issued decisions within business activities that must be followed, and pursued properly. A proper, and important observation includes how the Securities and Exchange Commission could have made sure more, or most corporate merger's had more liability. Therefore we must recognize the commitment of liability within risk, reward, and hard work to make a business workable, productive, and profitable with lawful, and logical liquidity.

The General Electric Corporation, General Motors Corporation, Ford Motors Company, the Enron Corporation, and WorldCom Corporation have been corporate businesses with large cash liquidity holdings, and reserves. A few of these corporations involved with other businesses have started subsidiary business operations, and corporate ventures with large amounts of equity, certain assets, and or cash that increases the volume of business earning potential. Another concentration of these businesses were started from their involvement in business merger's, and buyout's increasing their liquidity asset base that consisted of an access of cash, liabilities, and equity which became available within a long term stable business outlook. This availability of cash along with vast amounts of liabilities, and schedules for transactions including disclosers is part of most massive corporate business duties of management within financial responsibility. The result of liable business responsibilities or lawful survival for these (5) five corporations during 2010 is that (2) two no longer exist, and (2) two are struggling thru a serious financial crisis. This then gives us a small liability overview of loss within total asset value (c/o billions of dollars) which is "partly" how the present U.S. economy has been devalued with an economic crisis.

A conditional rate of business failure occurs from the factors of what happened to the Enron Corporation, the WorldCom Corporation, and how much work the Ford Motor Company will take to restructure. Considering 2009 this also includes General

Motors Corporation, and Chrysler Corporation including others observing various businesses in a bad American economic crisis. During 2006 Ford Motor Company reported an $11 billion loss that compiled some of their worse earnings in the company's history. Observing the same annual earning's review, the other two major American auto companies are having similar problems. This becomes the format of markets that consist of the business levels of production, projected cost, and expenses for a logical factor of projected earnings that don't always come easy. Their earnings at the Ford Motor Company, during 2006, and 2007 were below their projections, due to a lack of sales.

Another consideration within these businesses, and or publicly traded companies is how they view American investment communities of people, and most corporate equation issues of generated liquidity, and assets. Enron Corporation, and WorldCom Corporation where established in less than a decade with large conditions of "corporate merger cash", but their liability to earn capital was disastrous, and fraudulent. The United States government and most involved individual state governments most time work to regulate, and or appropriate the needs, and responsibilities of these massive corporations. This occasionally is helpful to the employees, the format of industry, and businesses including how the tax appropriated duties within government are to value a discipline of social liability. Contrary to this government logic, some corporations with enormous leveraging power went too far with certain investment's, and maybe not far enough with their liabilities within products, services, and or overall business.

Understanding the local economics of cities, towns, counties, states, and the applicable discipline of duty within the U.S. federal government, certain obligations of liability are vital. These liability, and economic issues consist of workable disciplines for all services, and duties provided by government, and the security for which these obligations apply. To maintain progress, this level of security for small and large businesses to work together on occasions is also a valued capacity of resource's for the American general public. This becomes the process of how tax dollars are generated, and then the people including the public, private businesses and government can format a solution for most all problems. Some of these markets, liabilities, and businesses have good sensible products, and services, but the worse example I understood was the products, and or services that Enron Corporation served to the American society. For "one" the corporation was considered an "Energy Trading" company, therefore it's complicated to say if they had a manufactured, or refined product to really sale. The other thing is that a vast amount of Enron business transactions, and commitments where with certain foreign countries, especially throughout complex parts of the Middle East.

During and after further review besides India, one of Enron Corporations biggest customer was the state of California. This became the issue where Enron Corporation controlled, and manipulated the public utility electricity market causing 10s of billions of dollars of fraud, and damage. This company Enron made, or had enormous amounts of money during certain business mergers, and then lost about 80% of their asset liquidity holdings in 2001. This becomes a severe problem for any business, and therefore even with Enron's involvement with "Portland-General Electric", this was a bad merger for the leveragability factors of income, and control of other businesses. Observing the unlawful conflicting facts this became a losing factor for the "Portland-GE" utility employees, and other American's with certain values of business, whom if possible had to restructure.

Unfortunately during the last 10 to 15 years around the 1990's, and the first few years of the 2000's decade, certain American businesses that provided important, and sometimes fairly good products on the market, have suffered liability, and business problems that are quite sad, and different. Certain businesses had liability problems that also consisted of vast amounts of manufacturing explosions which occurred throughout various different regions of the United States. This observation of business production liabilities has hit Northwest Indiana manufacturing hard (during a 10 year span) with about 5 or 6 severe fatal explosions that damaged the equipment, and injured people. One of the worse, or more complex fatal steel manufacturing explosions occurred (during 1996) at a steel plant in Portage, Indiana at the Bata Steel Corporation facility. This occurred when a welding sub-contractor for the steel plant was doing work by extracting a gas pipe with a flamed torch, and the explosion killed the (3) three men working, and injured many others. The massive explosion carried so must force that hundreds of feet of walls on (2) two of the large sides of the building where heavily damaged. Also 3 parts of the enormous 80 foot (in height) roof structure was ripped away, and destroyed!

A clear, and full consolidation of Bata Steel, and other steel mill, and manufacturing process plant explosions consisted of the cost of various equipment, the facility, and various injuries including the death of certain people employed that has been slightly devastating. This is a factual problem in American manufacturing liabilities where the company (including insurance contract agreements) must compensate for various cost, and or go to court for any, or most causes in the observed adjustable matter. Some of these companies only partly survived financially, and then a vast amount of businesses fell into bankruptcy. The Bate Steel Corporation facility in Portage, Indiana was a near complete loss, and disaster, although they did rebuild the facility. This becomes a sad complication in many ways for this Indiana region of America at the local, state, and United States federal government concern level for safe, and secured businesses. Also this includes the importance within production responsibilities that are questionable with needed corrections, logical revisions, and legislative disciplines.

In addition to worker safety issues the Indiana, and United States Departments of Labor should have had some logical understanding on how this could have been prevented. Alexis Herman was the United States Department of Labor Secretary during those years. Her, and the President Bill Clinton's agenda seemed to be concerned about management, and labor employment relations. This concern with the President Clinton Administration did not have too much aggressive concern of the OSHA (Occupation Safety & Health Administration), & MSHA (Mine Safety and Health Administration) safety issues. These were vital issues that intervened within the steel manufacturing, and coal mining industries of America. These important U.S. government facts are partly within the state, and U.S. federal Labor Department's concern, and responsible observation of liability.

Due to a few insecure mergers and buyouts the U.S. Department of Commerce, and the Securities and Exchange Commission should have been concerned more about conflicts of interest to control certain American industrial based businesses. It became questionable whether American or foreign ownership was important in America which becomes a sad, and complex problem. These conflicting foreign issues of ownership consisted of discrepancies upon how certain fatal accidents occurred before certain buyouts where pursued. This includes issues, and values within the concern of if government was doing a good enough job that is applicable to the regulated disciplines of these business activities (including insurance) in America. These concerns become vital to have safe, and lawfully productive work environments for the citizens, and any corporate buyout concerns that should have been in lawful order as it applies to the U.S. National Security, and Constitutional laws of the United States.

The liability cost before, and after certain tragedies including the issued duties of the United States Department of Labor has provided some good, and bad on the valued subjects of manufacturing liabilities. Throughout other parts of the United States such as in Danvers, Massachusetts (2006) a chemical plant exploded, and the facility was leveled clear to the ground. No one was injured in Danvers. Then another textile chemical plant in Morganton, North Carolina suffered an explosion with a chemical fire and at least 16 people were injured. This Synthron Inc. chemical plant in North Carolina with its headquarters in Paris, France was completely destroyed in Morganton. Also a chemical plant in Kansas City, Missouri (2006) had a "Propane tank" explosion that ignited other chemical tanks with enormous flames, and fires, but no one was injured. In Milwaukee, Wisconsin (2006) the Falk Corporation suffered an explosion that killed 3 employed people, and injured 46 other people working at the plant. This Milwaukee, Falk Corporation facility explosion was caused by a "Propane" tank problem, upon their manufacturing processes of metal gears, and other steel mechanical parts. Each and every one of these plant explosions caused damages, and the normal capacity of production, and business was delayed, and or shut down. This means their business liability especially with chemical processes (c/o propane) applicable to earning money for the products that they make, and sale will suffer. Upon this suffering within economic financial losses to the business, employees, and others including government, the necessity of liability issues will have to improve.

It is very complicated, but logical to understand what these damages to employees, equipment, and the facility's suffered completely. Another serious consideration is what this dose to the American economy, and money circulation including taxes, and additional concerns of insurance. These economic factors of insurance, and the operating capacity of a corporation that manufactures, and or that refines a chemical product, the cost factor, and other details become financially important. Contrary to this equation of accidents between 1995, and 2005 this has seem to be an exceptionally high rate of fatal, or nonfatal chemical explosions considering there has been plant explosions throughout the decades before the 1990s.

Another factual chemical explosion that occurred over the years of 2000 was at the (BP) British Petroleum Company (c/o London, England) Taxes City, Texas U.S. oil refinery plant. Previously this was an Amoco Oil Corporation facility which was the result of a buyout by British Petroleum Company during the late 1990s. During the plant operations within the month of March of 2005 the Texas City, Texas U.S. oil refinery suffered from its worse plant explosion in decades killing 14 employed people, and injured at least "100" others. Some of the people, and or surviving family's where still in, and out of certain court proceedings during 2007. This also includes the expenses of hospital procedures with doctors, and lawyers upon where some of the injured employees are still in, and out of hospitals with a variety of health problems. In addition, this includes the fact that some people have long term injuries, and then others died months, or years later with their newly complex health conditions. These work place injuries, fatalities, and the conditional damages have cost these refineries, manufacture's, various people, and the insurance company's heavily. Contrary to the diversified economics of other industries, American insurance businesses are making an effort to restructure or maintain the stability throughout their future in business. This therefore is a vital concern upon which these business matters and subjects within the American economy must be considered for within most future days, and years of safety, and industry production values.

Within the business format of insurance, and liability disciplines that the insurance company must pay for within their obligated insurance agreements, this includes the detailed property, insured people, and or assets within the conditional term of insured damages. Each time the insurance company pays these "clamed damage agreements" there is a factual balance sheet consisting of a negative financial adjustment, or loss to the insurance company. Theoretically the insurance companies, and industry operates on insurance payments (the input), and this becomes the insurance companies asset equity. A different objective also consist of the equity upon damages (the output), and this takes away from the insurance companies overall cash financial assets of management. This financial asset management issue of liability and equity has become a serious consideration for even the insurance industry that all of a sudden may have had more financial clam's then available cash assets. These concerns of asset liquidity and contingent liability requirements by law are vital to maintain their business duties, and operation. This has seemed to be a rare problem, but in some cases a vitally real one.

To take a financial assessment of the equity, and liabilities that have accumulated over the last decade, and a half approaching 2008, our American society of insurance, and manufacturing has consisted of excessive conflicting problems. Observing this problem within various businesses considering some natural disasters, these contingent factors have consolidated a financial problem. The financial loss of consolidation from insurance companies making payments for manufacturing facilities that where destroyed or damaged by explosions, or fire have made the insurance industry very nervous. Sure, this fact including the hurricane problem's in Louisiana, Mississippi, and Texas was another very expensive problem for all involved, but some agreeable commitments should be applicable.

The serious issue that the American insurance companies are possibly approaching is that more American insurance clam payments have started exceeding more than the American insurance company's may have available in business to compensate within equity. This also includes the cold shoulder effect of sadness when the uninsured people whom suffer losses, and then the insurance company will quickly explain "we have no, or any up-to-date insured coverage agreements with payments". Observing combined disasters, various states including the Gulf States (with Hurricane Katrina) all kinds of suffering has been devastating to the people. Then this becomes the real fact that most people, and professionals in the insurance business must protect the customers, and clients as lawful, and liable insurance company's. Contrary to disasters the future of business, and the values of equity are a continued issue of concern. This also becomes vital within employment opportunities and the effort within starting or expanding certain smaller businesses with insurance observing the future is in conflict, but some people will find a way to survival.

Illegal immigrants and international issues of conflict have factored some American businesses (c/o choice's) into a small uninsured environment of businesses. This is factual to the extent that various businesses have suffered a contingent great risk for long term economic stability. In some industries illegal immigrants providing cheap labor has occasionally turn into a business production expensive problem with damages from U.S. businesses not having educated American values to adequately help some American production. This is a vital conflict, considering some businesses, and people are having a difficult time restructuring to become fully insured, and or in financially functioning in good shape. Most personal, and business assets of the American society including health requires the inputs, and outputs of good insurance business decisions, and activities. In vital reality, it's more so just down right common sense, and good decision making a vast amount of the time.

Although the attacks of terrorism (c/o the 9-11 Terrorist Report) where conditionally covered with a percentage of help from the state government of New York, and distinctively the U.S. federal government, these personal losses effected numerous households. This was still observed as a domestic, and vital international issue of tremendously bad effects for the American people including various American assets. Just like most natural disasters the state or federal government may acknowledge that an area is in a "state of Emergency or Declared Disaster", and we as American citizens must understand, or recognize the safety, and valued money circulation requirements. In addition, the courts in mostly New York have recognized the liability, and compensation need (c/o lawsuits) of various first responders to this "9-11" terrorist attack. This therefore included how we must work together with supportive friends, constituents, government, and family members to overcome foreign related conflicts in America, even with law suite's being part of a solution.

Observing the executive, and legislative branches of the American system of government, and more so the judiciary some "insurance, and financial" company executive's, and employees have been prosecuted for their illegal practices. This seems even more conditional when a man in Chicago owns an insurance company, and he is worth hundreds of millions of dollars one day, and then months later he is prosecuted, and sent to jail penniless. In cases like this the employees also learn some bad business habits. Problem's like this leaves a hard truth and a discretionary agenda for others whom are victims, which eliminates incomplete justice being served. Not a whole lot of factual conversation is disclosed, pertaining the victim's though there was a lot of different discussions about conflicting matters. I have taken awareness of this because between insurance companies, the courts, and various people or businesses whom paid their rate of insurance appropriately, most vital decisions had to be made in various law case's with the courts. Then there was none, or very little service of liability disciplines applied, upon which additional problems where not complex, but caution, and or restructuring had to stay its course.

The executive branch of government observes the legislative branch making these laws, but then it's the important duty of the judiciary whom enforces them to keep people protected as best they can.

A couple other facts within business liability consist of certain markets that exist in the United States when various foreign people took control of certain major steel companies, and or corporations. The majority of these buyouts conducted by Wilber Ross (c/o ISG), and Lakshmi Mittal within the steel manufacturing region of Northwest Indiana occurred after certain accidents. As accidents questioned the disciplinary control of the steel industries management, and others (c/o foreign and American workers) with different conditions of liability, this became a valid concern. More attention slightly became a concern when a fatal accident occurred at U.S. Steel Gary Works which consisted of 3 Spanish sub-contractor employees on a cleaning crew that could not read, or understand the "Danger Signs". Their lack of misunderstanding caused them to suffocate to death in a gas chamber process near a blast furnace. Therefore these scientific industry standards with issues of caution have valid, and appropriate procedure to follow. In some concerns even an American high school drop out that had good intentions would have had enough knowledge to read, and evaluate this level of danger.

Observing addition liabilities within industry, and some nature conflicts of concerned condition, these issues can consist of fraudulent practices, and victimize people. This became the complacent problem within a lack of maintenance on the New Orleans waterway retention levees. Considering the factual concept of problems hear this made the Hurricane Katrina a tremendous disaster which provided wind, and more so deadly flood damages. It also affected various companies, and the liability insured oil company's equipment stationed in the Gulf of Mexico, and this has partly hurt some insurance companies, and others. Observing the flooding being the worse part of Hurricane Katrina it included

10s of thousands of cars, trucks, and houses (insured & uninsured), and a vast amount of small, and large businesses being severely damaged. This may not be counting the government assets that were damaged, but most all of them are insured. Understanding accidents or disasters of any kind, and the evaluation of restructuring, it doesn't say enough that insurance companies have their work cut out for them. Therefore in the future observing the 2000, 2010 and up to the 2020 decades, these issues may include legislature, and evaluated help from the American system of government, and citizens making the best decisions possible.

Approaching the years of 2010, and 2011 for the American markets within the oil industry, various conflicting problems have accumulated certain issues which have been disastrous. On April 20, 2010 another British Petroleum accident occurred in the Gulf of Mexico killing 11 oil rig workers, and injuring about 17 other employees. This was the British Petroleum (c/o Amoco / now BP) Company's 2nd bad accident in five years. Upon this April 2010 fatal explosion which was severe to the BP Deepwater Horizon Oil Rig (c/o the Transoceacn contractor) employees, the other real damage also became the day by day deep-water oil well outside of their normal drilling, and production system. The damaged oil rig burned, sank into the sea, and then continued to deposit oil from the broken underwater well into these American coastal waters off the shores of Louisiana. The oil reached land after around 25 days, and this continued to damage a vast amount of the preservation, and wildlife that exist in this Gulf Coast region. This access of uncontrollable oil flowing from a well underwater at about 5000 feet below the sea was pumping an estimated 250,000 gallons of oil a day into the water 50 miles off the coast of New Orleans.

Observing the corporate problems within the British Petroleum Company, and their CEO Tony Hayward upon which their production, and exploration problems of liability in America has compounded, these have become issues similar to other complex U.S. corporate businesses with occasional industrial disasters. The city of New Orleans, including other cities, towns, or parish's along the Louisiana coastal waters, and the British Petroleum Company will be struggling with this environmental disaster issue for a questionable length of time. Although some relief is becoming responsive, and productive certain internal soil, sand, and water contamination have been discovered in partial conditions. The Louisiana sea food fishing markets, and industry with at least hundreds or more vassal's were threatened for a variation of month's to come. Fisherman, and scientist on boat's, and vessels have been consistently testing the waters for these very complicated concerns about the quality of fishing produce that has been ruined, and the survival or recovery of other seafood commodities.

Nature's wildlife animals have been affected to the extent where some birds cannot fly, and mostly small fish can't swim properly upon the fact that some of these species are dying off form the oil contamination. With the help of environmentalist, and sea life care specialist (c/o veterinarians) a vast amount of these creatures have been rescued, and assisted back into their natural habitat. This disaster also includes the continued decisions of the United States federal government, and various appropriate agencies that have been active. These are cabinet members, and staff from the President Obama Administration working with the State of Louisiana Governor Bobby Jindal, and Billy Nungesser the "President of Louisiana's Plaquemines Paris" whom where a few of the people who made aggressive, and loud complaining effort in seeking federal help, awareness, and answers. Contrary to all levels of government in Louisiana, Mississippi, and Florida (as the state's waterways where effected) this problem is still the liability of the British Petroleum Company.

Considering the U.S. President Barack Obama (c/o the Department of Interior and the Environmental Protection Agency) this issue is causing aggravated opinion's about British Petroleum, and other oil company's professional integrity to solve these various types of oil well leakage problems. Observing the cleanup process Lisa Jackson of the U.S. EPA, and other environmentalist have debated issues pertaining a chemical dispersant to dilute oil that some considered could be more harmful to the environment. Another government issue consisted of Ken Salazar of the U.S. Department of Interior having the commission to observe the geologic settings throughout the ocean, and land that the oil will more than likely effect from state to state. This negative effect to different regional water's, and land have prompted other actions which had to be reviewed about the BP Company, and their activities with contractors like Transocean, and others.

Certain other government activities of concern consist of the President Barack Obama, his U.S. Coast Guard Commander of this "Oil Spill Disaster" Thad Allen, and the U.S. Attorney General Eric Holder which them, and others have been commanded to review factual concerns, and gather all evidence from the overall day by day conditions. Upon this resource of activities the Attorney General Eric Holder has made preparation to file a lawsuit. This includes information from the other U.S. Coast Guard officials investigating the events of the accident with the U.S. Bureau of Ocean Energy Management calling on BP employees, and a vast amount of other company's involved to testify. These testimonies are to help improve this offshore drilling process and a legal review about the events, and liability of their working conditional factors before, and at the time of the fatal explosion. These were important factors including other government issues, which may be part of at least 300 considered lawsuits. Therefore observing these issues, congressional hearings, and government concerns which are relevant, with details pertaining the oil clean up, and fatalities surrounding this BP Co disaster, a vast amount of industry, and government disciplines can be resolved, and evaluated for future enforcement.

These conflicting liability problems become almost as questionable as issues of foreign, and American buyout business transactions that have been slightly undisciplined for the American society. Upon the good, and more so bad of American corporate buyout issues, this vitally includes the conditional resource capacity of issues, and transaction's that occurred in Chicago when Amoco Oil Corporation was sold to the British Petroleum Company. Observing this buyout, and some lack of effort within better work standards within this concern of chemical refinery processes that carries over within how other Midwest U.S. businesses are coping with similar problems, these adjustments must be astute. These problems consist of the correct industry standards of revisions after a corporate buyout or merger, and the adjustments to this American business, and industry process of vital concern. Therefore this seems to have been another corporate buyout that has not worked very good for the citizens, industry, and the better means of capitalism within the society of the United States.

I believe one of the concluding subjects of business in the format of concern is valued within the discipline that public utility companies have liabilities and insurance on most all of their assets, and equipment. The public utility companies of America's different regions are monopolies in their own industry rights, and their markets for the residential, commercial, government, and other lawful customers. Some legal facts are held important within the United States Public Utility Company Holding Act., and this federal Act by the Congress and the United States government, observes the utility companies with the lawful rights to serve a regions regulated utility needs. Also another vital factor is the economics, and financial disciplines of the "Utility Holding Company", and each discipline of a public utility company. Observing this and the understanding of how public utility companies operating disciplines work, is partly within the coordination of the state, and the federal laws. This format of disciplined procedures includes government officials, and public service issue commitments to a region. There are most time engineering, and or professional commitments including regional disciplines that become important. Other professional commitments occur routinely over the years which, includes various changes for most needed utility equipment operating systems, and infrastructure upgrades. Therefore this is part of most Public Utility Holding Company requirements.

Another resource of Public Utility Company disciplines becomes important when these businesses find themselves with vast amounts of equipment problems, and damage's from different weather conditions. Besides weather, some utility equipment problems comes from occasional professionals that don't provide design commitments (accessing utility crew's) to their work duties to upgrade, apply engineered designs, and manage engineering system's such as SCADA control processes. This also is recognized with intervention that becomes the aggressive operating processes to keep all systems completely in order, and therefore any outside negative conflicts such as Enron Corp. is, and became a tremendous industry problem. A vast amount of American public utility electric company's where negatively affected contrary to their upgrading, coordinating, or managing issues when the Enron Corporation intervened with their destructive energy trading business transaction. The "Holding" company status is part of a public utilities liability cost with the company, contractors, and customers that is applicable to "active utility infrastructures" for safe, logical services, and responsible duties for the general public. This then separates utility companies from other businesses due to their commitment to an overall region as it applies to financial matters, income earnings, and the lawful discipline of services.

Within the consideration of utilities, and infrastructures the United States consist of a vast amount of government (municipal, state, and U.S. regional) owned industrial utility process facilities. This is a format within the Public Monopoly concept, and or issues that the United States government helps provide within the U.S. Post Office, and the Internal Revenue Service, and a few others such as operating dams, and toll roads. These U.S. government duties considering certain public monopolized business procedures such as within the U.S. Post Office, and the Internal Revenue Service are held with lawful standard's, and are closely reviewed by government. Contrary to public monopolies this also more so consist of certain government facilities that control the process of dams to regulate levels of water, or storm water, and certain conditions of the infrastructure similar to the highway, and toll road operations which includes some gated systems. These are process conditional issues to produce electricity, retain water, and keep citizens safe, and directed with mapping signs which are government projects, and duties of liability. This also includes facilities to control the flow of storm water (c/o the U.S. Army Corps of Engineers) process procedures, and or to maintain roadways, and bridges. These infrastructure concerns and public monopolies are, and should be conducted within their budget coordinated disciplines for the highest elite standards, and levels of liability. Therefore with these responsibilities that are appropriated to the American general public, and citizens we can observed a well-developed society.

Different concerns also exist within more so some of our American infrastructure, and utility concerned issues. These infrastructure and American utility components are occasionally in bad, and or obsolete condition considering how productive (c/o expanding or descending) their operating capacity levels of public need or access exist. These state and federal infrastructures are also valued with the importance of annual budget concerns which may require more effective regulative disciplines in the future. This liability issue, and observation can be noticed when certain parts of an enormous amount of cities, and towns near rivers, are causing "hundreds of millions", if not billions of dollars of damages every year. The vast amount of damages from flooding, and cresting rivers with or more so without dam's, and levees that are obsolete have been a part of this deprived government infrastructure subject. Most structured dams, and levees have a severe need for repairs, and upgrades which is part of this vital budget, and managing concern throughout the United States. Therefore the taxpayers liability has become a big issue of will it, and the government do the best they can to keep the people, and their livable assets, and families safe, and productive? The logical answer is very complex compared to the important decisions of business, engineering, other occupations, and the American system of government in the future.

Business And Corporate Liabilities
(3)

CHAPTER THREE
(3)

The United States Library of Congress

Business And Corporate Liabilities
(3)

The American society and the world that we live in consist of many businesses, and corporations that provide different, and diversified products, and services that lawfully must maintain liability. These corporations, and even the small and somewhat large public, or private businesses use the best and most logical skills to establish liability. These issues of liability are for marketing the products, and services they provide to the general public, or clients to earn money. This vital format most times, includes being able to pay the applicable, and logical taxes of the state, and federal government. The United States government, including most of the public, and private businesses of America were compiled within expansion when things went well. This lead a vast amount of corporations throughout America to have discipline that applied their various duties, and achievements for over the last 100 years. Then therefore they had to consolidate these good and bad times of changing liabilities of experience, and efficiency.

Understanding the best businesses and sometimes the effort within good businesses that look the worse, before correction's in a year, from "time to time" they usually understand that the total best outcome requires workable commitments. The disciplines of workable commitments is like the hardest working scholars, or the most skilled athletes that work with others, and then they work to improve in all other way's. Sometimes luck, or skill is acceptable, and compared to the (first) 1st time of ever driving a spike in the ground, and a person finds, and discovers a rich oil well. Either or, luck is not a good factor (c/o interesting results) as our American society has observed along with certain guidelines which consist of the most productive thing's, but the best values consist of a format of hard work, and commitment.

Most markets of the United States for years have consisted of transportation, entertainment, utilities, healthcare, energy, banking, investment banking, insurance, telecommunication, computer science, agriculture, and farming. Now added to these markets, is the different, and diversified arbitration of internet services, with the exception of a few other computer products for personal, and industry use. The largest market with complexities is now within the expanding business arbitration of "information technology" that will consist of various changing factors as the years, and decades of 2000 go on.

Other vital markets consist of farming within agriculture, and non-farming commodities that become important subjects for the diversified markets of America. This also includes professions that provide scientific disciplines, and studies within the professions and occupations of architecture, engineering, construction, computer programming, and internal medicine. The format of occupations, and professions is recognized in places such as hospitals, water and wastewater treatment plants, chemical refineries, diversified manufacturing facilities, utility companies, diversified banking facilities, and investments banking firms, accounting firms, engineering, and or architecture firms. This also includes others whom are valued with scientific principal studies including technological research in laboratories conducted by diversified professionals working on certain projects. Otherwise there is a market for almost every concept, and issue of life in America including the needs of professionalism, and liabilities of all forms of our diversified businesses, and government. Observing these businesses, and their established management procedures most all have different levels of a business, and liability format to appropriate success in their valued sectors of a market.

Most American corporations, and various businesses have an established condition of publicly owned business duties, and activities that are quite different from most privately owned businesses. This is the format, and consideration of the businesses that are considered appropriate when public investments can increase the business operations to capacity levels with expansion, and efficiency. General Electric Corporation has a vibrant presents as an international business, but most of their business is done, and pursued in America. International markets, and corporation's with the likes of British Petroleum Company (PLC), and a few others have gain large amounts of good, and more so bad interest in American business. This observation within the capacity of public companies in America, which effects various private companies, and businesses have a vital concern to keep certain good activities logical with some local businesses productive. Usually some of these private businesses (c/o opinions) turn into publicly traded company's when all, or most things are pursued, and go well within the provisions of marketing a product, or service. This is the business offering process of financial markets within stocks, bonds, and the lawful business concerns within small, and large investors.

Small, large, and what is considered as international investors increases the capital wealth of certain companies at very high percentages within the time, and equity created from their business performance. Sense 1990 the United States has fallen short on enforcing the laws as it applies to "international investments, and international terrorism". American investors, and business owners have a logic within all the laws that apply to their business disciplines that should be considered, and valued productively by all other people, and citizens including various small and large businesses including corporations. A vast amount of franchise businesses are now from 1990 thru 2009 becoming foreign owned, and this is a conflict for certain U.S. Constitutional laws, and U.S. National

Security values. This diversified marketing process, and various levels of procedures also consist of the United States Securities and Exchange Commission (SEC) rules, regulations, and laws. Understanding these times of conflicting business transactions, certain problems where part of complacent government in America that occasionally supported people, and business from enemy county's, over some of their own valued American citizens considerably as it applies to business.

Observing various terrorist, and U.S. Anti-Trust law conflicting business "liability" attacks against government, and some citizens this has caused American workable standards to be a loss and victimizing people to be vulnerable. This may have been affected by complacent work duties that have allowed American business professionals, and certain officials of government to be put into unworkable managing conditions. During the years of 2000 to 2008 the circulation of SEC chairman's being Auther Leveit, Harvey Pitt, William Donaldson, and then Chris Cox have caused suffering with critical conflicts of not keeping public investors secured in a timely fashion of liable financial security. Between the financial criminal conflicts of the 1990s like with Bernard Madoff, Ameritech Corp, Enron Corp, WorldCom Corp, and the concern of some unlawful international investment issues, these concerns may have frustrated these SEC Chairman's which seem to be a tuff office, and position to hold from 1995 to 2008. Contrary to the fact within all being said, and more so done it is also just as "vitally" important to understand applicable commitments "to and from" the state, and federal U.S. Constitutional laws. This also applies to the courts, and their judicial powers with various people in government which is occasionally a conflict, and can be complacent by certain people.

People as investors observe U.S. Securities and Exchange Commission matters with diversified understanding of the different good, and bad examples of those businesses who's income earnings are slightly complex. These businesses such as within the Microsoft Corporation, Dell Computer Corporation, and more so the indifference of WorldCom Corporation, the Enron Corporation, and a few others are known to have divers businesses. Considerably, company's like the General Electric Corporation, Eastman Kodak Corporation, and various types of individual's upon others have used this format of marketing, and investing to consolidate earning additional liquidity within their business activities. Jack Welch used this process truly well with General Electric Corporation during the 1980s to increase market share, and their values of GE corporate liquidity. The strategy at General Electric consisted of GE making investment capital gains from large investments, but this also was occasionally part of a merger, or buyout process to restructure the company with GE management to make it profitable. This becomes appropriate SEC values within the logical business priority's, and earnings that corporations have within reasons to protect their investments, and future operating capacity.

Enron Corporation consisted of large, small, old, and young investors which theoretically most all of them involved suffered when their publicly traded stock hit the bottom financially. A few employees, and top management officials did leave the company early on, and sold their stock for cash with one official taking away an estimated $200 million dollars. WorldCom Corporation investor's, and certain employees suffered the same way, but company's like Dell Computer Corporation was established for greater stability. Enron, and WorldCom where corporations that where heavily involved in buyout (junk bond) transactions, but their liquidity was tremendous before failure due to illogical top level managing, and unlawful procedures. The Dell Computer Corporation also as a fairly new company has endured most recent stock market liquidity factors of good and bad market trading days in the American financial markets of resourceful business. Dell Computer Corporation with their founder / CEO Michael Dell is a business unlike some other corporate concerns that was started with a product that made good sense to the American consumers. Therefore common products with values and lawful business practices have been a vital factor of long term American business progress, similar to the progress that Bill Gates made with Microsoft Corporation.

When small productive businesses, or the old, and or exhausted private businesses observe certain levels of management, marketing, contingent liabilities, and possible investor considerations these issues are taken serious for any good, and bad reasons necessary. The United States government observes, and understands this lawful concern within how the American general public can observe the best diversified changes when the corporations management has to make vital decisions. Microsoft Corporation, and Dell Computer Corporation where within appropriate planning of this format of a public offering process, but Microsoft Corporation had different products that were IBM compatible during the 1980s before a vast amount of others. Actually Microsoft Corporation grew from one major stock trading exchange to the largest which is the New York Stock Exchange. International Business Machine (IBM), like the former Digital Equipment Corporation have worked towards certain disciplines with products, and some computer services over the years, and this was their productive competitive edge that was excepted in most financial markets.

The real competitive edge became diversified with Microsoft Corp, Netscape Corp., and others pursued conflicts in the courts. This was the factual conflict which consisted of patent rights legal disputes in the courts, and other concerns to manage controlled ownership of these products. This was applied when Microsoft Corporation and Netscape Corporation had a legal split, and law dispute over the development of the computer operating "browser" that was invented, and developed to digitize computer programs.

Contrary to Microsoft, and Netscape Corporation's skills to develop, and created a new market for computer software, and the operating systems that interface with more types of programs, this made computers user friendly. These became helpful components of the internet, and computer data processes that were still being worked on observing certain arbitrary issues. Considerably, this took computer, and software purchases from "hundreds of thousands", to "hundreds of millions" if not a billion sold. These conditions of business, and improvements of workable disciplines of computer liabilities took hold of investor, and market awareness. This is how they worked their way thru the different financial market exchanges such as the NASDAQ, and the New York Stock Exchange apart from certain differences at the American Stock Exchange.

A vast amount of commodities used in various corporate products are traded on the Chicago Board of Trade Exchange, and the New York Mercantile Exchange. These commodity trading markets like some other commodity exchange's trades non-durable commodity items. These non-durable commodities are important by-products used in the manufacturing of computers, cars, gas, wood structures, steel components, chemicals, paper, different medicines, foods, and other materials, and products. To understand corporate cost, and the importance of non-durable commodities these large quantity purchase, and price factors consist of a responsibility to buy raw materials which becomes critical to be used properly, and productively as manufacturing buy-products. Thousands of businesses, and corporations buy or purchase these diversified commodities for good logical use, and or sales as durable, and non-durable items. Observing these values, a diversion within bad corporations like Enron Corporation, and even WorldCom Corporation, consist of these various purchase disciplines that where not completely applied. These businesses with their Chief Executive's Ken Lay, and Bernie Ebbers including other business officials, worked thru these company's receiving enormous amounts of money, and corporate stock. Therefore within their stock holdings, and lack of good business discipline these issues became evident, and then most valued concerns of business, and their "considered" products, and services suffered. Certain food company's like General Mills, or pharmaceutical company's like Merck & Company did not suffer bad due to market reactions, and their disciplines to operate a corporation in a productive way maintained stability.

The observation of a vast amount of people would say that Bill Gates, the founder of Microsoft Corporation has earned hundreds of millions of dollars, or more than a billion dollars from the expansion of the DOS (disk operating systems) invention from Microsoft products. His earnings of more than a billion dollars from his hard work of developing the disk operating system products at Microsoft Corporation became factually vital to all IBM compatible computer operating systems. Non-durable goods, and liability cost are considered in their computer products which includes instruction books, and diversified materials like plastic for various diskettes. The Microsoft Corporation has exceeded most of its business, and product expectations, and this has established value within this American corporation of economic, and market discipline. The expectations of these other corporations within Enron, and WorldCom apart from Microsoft became evident within losses due to the good of money, and more so bad products, and or services that "only" looked like a good market trading issue. Considering these market resources, and business issues of success, and more so the levels of failure which was lurking, this destroyed investors, and employees. Then the corporate cash liquidity (c/o even dividend reduction) factors within certain long term business concerns were not part of a secured business.

Both Enron, and WorldCom Corporation's where established, and started from corporate mergers, and large stock conversions within corporate buyout cash transactions. This also consisted of the occasional good, the severely bad junk bonds, and hostile corporate takeovers throughout the "Securities and Exchange Stock and Bond markets" with business procedures, and transactions. Within the fact of a business achieving market capitalism with effective growth there are lawfully good products, and services involved most all the time. This has become evident in Microsoft, Netscape, Dell, and oil company's like ExxonMoble, and others. Also besides the employed people enjoying their work, and job the general public is, and becomes the satisfied constituent with what they are spending or investing their money on to buy. The Enron Corporation, and the WorldCom Corporation had very complicated products, and or services that I don't even think "they knew" what the businesses where offering "did"; except provide an investment dollar circulation, and salaries. WorldCom, and Sprint Corporation in 1999 tried to announce a $115 billion dollar merger, but the United States government regulators with certain foreign regulators from Europe said they would oppose the merger due to "Anti-Trust" law reasoning. The deal was called off. Upon these business issues, and most government regulators it's important to remember an "Energy Company" or a "Communications Company" are not registered "Financial Brokerage Companies" within how they conduct business within the service provisions of "economics, and utilities".

Both of these troubled corporate businesses considering Enron, and WorldCom had so many employees, certain investors, technology issues, and resources of cash involved, it's real to say they had the wrong idea about a few of the more important things. Some of the resources of investors and employees were inherited from certain merger transactions, and considerably moving logical or conflicting management out, considering some whom were reassigned, or those that resigned. The billions of dollars that these corporations started with "then lost" domestically, and internationally was, and could have been partly the start, and success of potentially 50 or more other smaller private businesses all over the United States. One company that was created during an expansion of the computer internet market was the America Online Company which found prosperous success within business liabilities to earn money in a new, and fairly productive market. This process of business concerns also includes a questionable tax base, and need for more security within the people of America's (2000) existing obsolete utility infrastructures although good market expansions became complex. Considering the occurrence of problems, this is where investors or some other businesses like internet service providers, and especially the American system of government had to consider improved or better regulated duty's. These are the facts within the possibility of helping other companies that may have needed, or could have used certain financial resources better.

As Americans observed "Financial Brokerage Company's, and other businesses like Time Warner Incorporated, and the America Online Company (AOL) during 2000 which agreed too, and completed a financial merger / buyout transaction, "this deal", and agreement was worth more than $150 billion dollars. This buyout / purchase of Time Warner Inc was led by AOL Company Inc. CEO Steve Case, and investors like Ted Turner of AOL Inc which had achieved financially productive business, and market progress from 1991 to the year 2000. Marc Seriff, and Steve Case made the AOL internet business computer service operation "very productive" by incorporating their service for both IBM compatible, and Apple compatible computer internet users. The factual liability within logical long-term market / business resources is that Time Warner Incorporated was the company that held liquidity, and market capital business requirements. The AOL Company made this merger / buyout transaction possible, but their newly found investment market capital wealth went dry with the AOL - Time Warner Company Inc. reporting a loss of over $95 billion dollars in 2002. This was a historical loss for any American company, and from 2004 through 2009 starting with the former Time Warner CEO Richard Parsons, and his business leadership, the business transaction was reversed with AOL Inc. then becoming a corporate spin-off issue.

Considering WorldCom Corporation, and AOL Incorporated, these businesses where in similar markets upon which AOL Incorporated had a productive, but complex "partner" within the company Time Warner Incorporated. Ted Turner (c/o Turner Broadcasting & Company) as the Chairman of the board of AOL, was the lifeline of this business concept of overall existence for AOL Incorporated. This gave AOL Incorporated additional liquidity with financial operating stability, and liability to survive the complex markets throughout the "dot COM internet" expansion of companies. These internet companies, and their arbitration was tremendous, but an enormous amount of this new concept of businesses did not survive immediately in various American markets. Therefore the liability of these American internet, and telecommunication companies during this decade of business where just as some described it; being "a bubble that did not hold air". Upon this factor of certain internet companies that did hold air in the bubble, an important factor was the enter-phase of modems, and the telephone companies with pricing factors, but some major telephone businesses had their own problems as well. Considering this market liability issue of increased phone line users the regional telephone company's seem to compile excessive volume capacity with cost evaluated problems that took time to solve.

The concept of new expanding markets (c/o the dot .Com bubble) also had effects on the mix between the former Ameritech Corp, Southwestern Bell Corporation (SBC), and AT&T Corporation which included a few others. This was an important example within evaluated business, and resource decisions within the American system of government to expand regulation for liability, and companies to expand innovated business activities. These business, and government decisions about the new conditions of the internet, and additional upgrades of communication systems are business concerns that are providing the indifference within America struggling with these changing conflicts, and their values of liability. This becomes relevant as it applies to the Federal Communication Commission (FCC), and more so internet computer companies, including the concept within networking of computers from the former Digital Equipment Corporation. This gave the FCC more regulated concerns within an expanding market, including the use of modem's for information technology.

The American Telephone & Telegraph Corporation has also developed a market that consist of enormous products, and services that has led to AT&T mergers with other smaller productive corporations. Dobson Communication Corporation has established a merger agreement with AT&T which includes the Dobson Comm. Corp. "Cellular One" brand of wireless communication systems to become part of a combined resource to expand the logic of innovated business at AT&T. This is the format of AT&T increasing innovation along with competitive issue (c/o Comcast Corporation) that lawfully, and aggressively occur in business. These businesses including public utility companies have endured many good, and bad American economic times, and therefore a majority of the hard work including these innovated concerns provides a level of corporate American liability.

In retrospect, other types of businesses have had to take awareness of how these changing times, and liability conditions will effect most business operations. These effects are applicable to the general public within observation of communication, media, and other various markets of managing disciplines between people, employees, business, and government that is vital. Even new company's like Dell Computer Corporation, and a few others (being different from communication companies) have not suffered badly, but they have valuable decisions to continue to make concerning future business astute. These values consist of the good, and bad of various sectors of business and technology company's which contrary to their financial, and social level of satisfaction, there are important values to maintain the liability, and issues of overall lawful management disciplines. Microsoft, *Saturn, and General Electric upon other corporations that do have logical products, are more so established for long-term growth, similar to major telephone company's. Then these businesses are very much so part of the United States Gross Domestic Product (GDP) measurements, and they are long term valuable assets to the American economy. These levels of long term business are also part of the discipline of agriculture, and farming sectors of business that appropriate the diversified GDP rates.

Another sector of business, and products such as from conditional farm crops, and livestock animals is the different concentration of foods, restaurant items, and even the format of evaluated foods in hospitals that are vital markets of professionally divers liability. Hotels and other establishments throughout America that accommodate dinning people with food preparation services are another resource within markets where standards, and liabilities are established. Some hotels have changed to the extent that a full service restaurant, kitchen, and food storage operation may not exist, and this gives them a lower food cost, and operating budget to stabilize earnings. This applies to the Gross National Product (GNP) rates. The GNP measures the rate of people being served and or sold these products in these establishments. Understanding the excess of most general public needs these business products, and facilities consist of the effective good standards of business, and corporate values that maintain disciplines of responsible liability for the volume of people served.

Food service corporations, and hotel service corporations have restructured or changed over the years just as other large corporations have. In the auto industry Saturn Corporation was established from General Motors Corporation with good products within liability, but due to bad economic conditions in 2009 the company was shut down. This is where market stability has loss various product resources, but compared to food which is a vital, and different consumer product the government more so even helps needy families buy this vital product of necessity. This state and more so federal welfare program with the purchase of larger calculated amounts of food stamp orders is a program that offsets food business earnings, and provides society a beneficial resource. Also this slightly helps the food industry, and people. Corporations like Hilton hotels, and Best Western hotels have diversified locations to fit the different budgets of people, and their arrangements of traveling, and this helps accommodate issues of wasteful spending. Therefore the excessive business procedures "professionally" that these business matters in the future will require, is more stable all around surroundings of discipline. These are also professional liabilities that consist of products, and services with productive values for responsible American business liabilities.

Healthcare, and pharmaceutical products, including the business professionals that depend on these pharmacy products consist of factors within government, and professional liabilities of discipline. The people of the general public depend on a vast amount of medical products that the American "pharmaceutical, or drug companies" provide. This even more so applies within the coordinated effort of the United States "Food and Drug Administration" (FDA) to regulate the liability factors of these medical industry products with standards. These food, drug, and beverage industry concerns (c/o even water), and the vital consideration of other public health prevention issues, or products are very important within the factors of these liabilities. Observing these business liability issues to be concerned with the format of internal medicine, and all people young, and old are the focus of FDA decisions, and issues to provide public safety within various products. This concept of business includes even when, and how government, and the resource of people use their accessible resources, and make the best recommended decisions within possible good leadership in government, professionalism, and business. Their decisions should always make this, and other duties a valued logic. Observing this within a business format of conditions, it is important with most commend sense levels of logic that all things that play a role, and have an important role within liability, these values are to be supported or evaluated by dependable market resources.

The corporate Issues, and businesses such as within the American Pharmaceutical Company's similar to Merck & Company, Ely Lilly & Company, and Pfizer Incorporated are valuable corporate businesses for the markets of internal medicine professionals, and the American general public. Even the over-the-counter sectors of pharmaceutical businesses like Johnson & Johnson Inc., Chatten Company Inc., and the Colgate-Palmolive Corporation are businesses that provide high levels of liability within the products they make, and sale for valuable health care levels of importance. This becomes the importance of the healthcare hygiene products, and even low dos medications that are most times less harmful then prescribed medicines. The other reasons why these markets are important is because the doctors that prescribe certain medications that pharmaceutical company's develop, manufacture, and sale "do so" with the logical understanding, and evaluation of diagnoses that are given to most doctor's patients, and the people. Another reason of lawful concern is that the Food and Drug Administration of the United States government formerly evaluates, researches, and conducts test on all the pharmaceutical products that these companies plan to put on the market. These scientific disclosures and studies between the pharmaceutical companies, and the United States government are within the professional guidelines of the American people within being the patients for these internal medicine products.

Considering internal medicine and diverse medication issues, is a worldwide issue, American standards are still vital. These become the doctor prescribed values of medicine, and or healthcare awareness issues that American people, and others throughout the world and society are given for a sickness. Understanding these medications are a disciplined process, they are usually directed for use at home, within doctor's offices, and in all hospitals. This occasionally includes a few medications in other places when an emergency response has concerns, but doctors have to approve even emergency medicine "most times" after an "Emergency Transport", and arrival to a hospital. The market and professional duties between people and professionals in the hospitals or as paramedics must understand these factors of liabilities, and scientific principals with specifications. These become some of the well-developed American society duties, and procedures that are different from other good, and bad issues of international medicine concerns, and the proper use of medications. Therefore all the medical attention within what kind of prompt care is needed for people becomes part of these diversified emergencies. Understanding this, and the concept of injuries, illnesses, and other circumstantial patient requirements are factored as relevant for what may and dose have need for a healthcare concern, or medical solutions.

The American society of product's and the service's that apply to doctors of internal medicine have a vital dependency on the markets, and liabilities of American pharmaceutical companies, and their products including professional services. Over the hundreds of years, and vast amounts of companies, the markets with issues of pharmaceutical drug products have provided valid conditions of efficiency for most sick people, and the provision of serious illnesses. This format of liabilities is, and was established for all ages of people from infant baby's, the middle aged, and the concept of senior citizens. Considering this provision of diversified appropriations of cost, and medical services with doctors, it also consist of specialized medical communities with research that is an outlined discipline of all internal medicine.

Corporations providing drugs and pharmaceutical products understand different specialties of internal medicine in general practice. Then understanding the company and doctors prescribing medicine this is the way that the corporate products have liability, and dependability that maintains a formal good, or command grade of lawful use. Observing this, there is occasionally bad product liability issues that from "time, to time" may not go right with the understanding that medications have side-effects, different allergenic effects on certain people, or medicine that was developed improperly. Considering this the medicine dose not perform good, and this provides misguided (possible prognosticated) symptoms, or problems within additional illness issues. Then these become illness issues of concern where additional doctor / patient issues of caution must be reviewed, and considered.

Various issues of liability are the things that occasionally hurt the drug maker (c/o MD Physicians), or pharmaceutical companies such as how the Anti-Depressant drug Zoloft caused additional health problems, and some fatalities. The drug Zoloft was made by Ely Lilly & Company, and therefore due to legal proceedings the company like others suffered a slight financial loss, and then the company discontinued the product. It is occasionally common that corporations have a product that they must review within the factors of the pursuit of design and liability, just as Ford Motor Company during the late 1990s had a problem with (SUV) trucks that occasionally flipped over while making sharp turns. This becomes the liability of product issues that are widely considered for purchase, then these are vital issues to be observed with corrections for effective liability of corporate products, and the people's concern of safe, and useful product disciplines. Therefore most relevant duties by the U.S. government, including state regulators to outline safety, or proper and or professional use of various diversified products in America has requirements of lawful logic.

The observation of corporate and business arbitration in the United States is the consolidation that products, services, and liabilities are understood so that the people can logically see, understand, invest, or make purchases with levels of comfort in a lawful evaluation of agreements. Though investments might be discretionary in private companies, the whole sale buy, and retail sale process (upon supply, and demand) is part of this relevant business duty of transactions, and processes. Arbitrary disputes are included especially within 3, 4, or more individual businesses that apply to corporate issues. Then the underwriting from investment brokerage firms that may create a government disciplinary concern within businesses, and solitude consist of a vast amount of people being effected. This is considered for a long-term level of progress, although this has been lacking discipline during the first decade of 2000. These problems before hopeful corrections is similar to understanding that General Motors (contrary to the government) could not help a good car company like Saturn Corporation because they were one of last un-matured subsidiary businesses established before the 2008 economic crisis. In the reduction process Oldsmobile was eliminated also. These are the agreements, and disagreements upon settled disputes within the format of issued priorities of business. Then the American public's interest within General Motors became, how would they save their budget, and resource of liquidity, and earnings? Due to new proposals of vehicle emission laws this became applicable to the interest between other conditions of business, government, and society with future value.

How productive a corporation or business can arbitrate a product, and services within a market, or most business agreements, and or disagreements with the best, or most proper, and productive decisions is the determination of the business establishing the best output, and results. All businesses from restaurants, hospitals, hotels, manufactures, and other establishments that understand this value of business is observed as a very important factor, and subject. This is why the United States Constitutional laws and sacrifices of government, and business becomes important on the state, and federal level when solitude applies to decisions. Then any changes or other procedures that have legal effects have guidance, and then this applies from management with resources to appropriate the best possible solutions. Usually observing government working together the small, and large businesses can help the proper enforcement of the United States Constitutional laws, including "local, and state laws". This also applies to the "individual state government's" Constitution's with concern of most American business values of logic, and most all established provisions by government. These business values are also occasionally found in some "Articles of Incorporation". Considering the vital importance of these resources, the American people and consumers then can achieve a vast amount of satisfaction, and values that are required with financial, and livable security.

Understanding the enforcement of the U.S. Constitutional laws, and other governed regulation, some corporations have achieved restructuring within certain business activities. This includes the businesses and individuals involved with certain high management grade levels of responsibility. During 1982 the Continental Bank of Chicago filed for bankruptcy, but unlike some other businesses they never prospered again, accept as a "trust company" under the Federal Deposit Insurance Corporation. This consolidated issue, and problem was within the good, and more so bad liabilities of bank lending delinquency's (c/o managing) that caused financial harm within bank estimated earnings. In additional reference during the 1970s, but more so 1975 the Chrysler Corporation suffered a threat within bankruptcy due to air pollution regulation, and conflicting auto sales. Within this format of the automobile industry with Chrysler Corporation including Lee Iacocca (the former CEO) whom factored a level of hard work within liabilities, he was then able to restructure this automobile company to normal economic earnings. This was a different sense of effort then during the years of 2000 when the company had reorganized several times with a factor of good, and bad earnings. These efforts where achieved with formatted decisions, including slightly complex merger agreements with certain company's, and business people. Observing these businesses of complex decisions that include restructuring being a part of the American system of checks, and balances with good products, or services that suffered, America can be productive with better levels of responsible discipline.

Apart from the American steel manufacturing company's (c/o some chemical plants after 2000) whom were being hit the hardest with fatal explosions, and financial liabilities during the 1990s, the pharmaceutical businesses, and companies have been slightly more stable. With the consideration of Ely Lilly & Company making the drug Zoloft, and then having several "Product Liability" law suits brought against them, the company seemed to do well understanding the format of their other products. These other product lines of productive medicine that held good on their financial balance sheets have proven to be vital to their business. This format of achievements by the Ely Lilly & Company, Johnson & Johnson Inc., and even everything from food to tobacco companies, and including aircraft manufactures have struggled or worked to achieve business progress. Contrary to the ups, downs, and reality of the automobile industry in America, these businesses have found productive outcomes. One tobacco company which is RJ Reynolds Tobacco Company is still holding a record for trying to recover (c/o 1988) from one of the largest corporate takeovers in history, and this is part of various conflicting issues of American business. Considering these facts of prosperity this is observed when the logical values of hard work, commitment, and consistent disciplines are applied to certain American individual businesses, and market sectors of industry.

The Markets, Liabilities, & Corporate Merger's
(A good and bad formal issue)
(4)

CHAPTER FOUR
(4)

The United States Library of Congress

The Markets, Liabilities, & Corporate Merger's
(A good and bad formal issue)
(4)

Within the observation, and fact of the American financial markets, certain business liabilities, and corporate mergers have been "a discretion of the volatility" that sometimes seems to never end for the good of certain financial markets, and this includes their associated companies, and businesses. This financial market, and resource of business concerns consist of individual, corporate, and even government investors. Considering the financial liability of 1 or 2 corporations, and or business mergers, including hostile corporate take-over issues, this has provided the American markets, and economy some good, and bad issues. Corporate American buyout transactions for some people, and mostly investors that see the financial cash concerns, becomes a relevant capital gain issue. A vast amount of people understand that there is products, services, and liabilities that keep these businesses working with investment dollars at "good, and occasional bad" rates of efficiency.

Most upper management officials of a corporation, and or wealthy investors that sometimes do consider the merger, or buyout format of business resource procedures within 1, or 2 companies, observe cost concerning the good, or bad products, services, and earnings upon what could be capital gains. This also includes the all-around conditions of satisfaction that can be restructured, or gained from the short, or long term investments within a public corporation. These issues are the determination factors that can be observed for potential earnings, and business development issues of the business being purchased or bough-out. In retrospect, improving the conditions of a reorganizing companies management this is usually a determination to apply a better format of operating conditions to the present companies duties of managing, and other details for productive efficiency. This also includes the companies operating conditions within products, or services, and how this requires a formal condition of hard work, and commitment which may apply to severe changes in management. Contrary to the importance of business commitments this is also an occasional delight to investor's, and the employees of certain companies, or the relevance for certain businesses to provide a more prosperous future.

During the late 1980s the consolidation of corporate hostile take-over activity was vigorous. These corporate mergers, and take-over issues consisted of corporations like Phillips Petroleum Company, Eastman Kodak Company, Sterling Drug Corporation, Polaroid Corporation, Exxon Corporation, Mobil Oil Corporation, Del-Monte Food Corporation, and RJ Reynolds Tobacco Company including others. General Electric Corporation, Mesa Petroleum, and investment bankers such as *Kohlberg, Kravis, Roberts, & Company (KKR), Donaldson, Luskin, & Jenrette Inc (DLJ), and a shrewd few others were responsible for billions if not a trillion dollars or more in take-over bids. These financial activities within a vicious (Junk Bond) market during a period of about 8 to 10 years during the late 1980s consisted of good, and bad corporate long-term security values. These where part of various transactions, that consolidated different liabilities for corporate investments in America. This consolidation of conflicting liabilities have given conflict to a vast amount of American corporations including their investors which sometimes have observed fraud, and issues of U.S. National Security concerns.

Years later William Donaldson of DLJ investment bankers took a leave of absence when he was appointed by the President George

Bush Administration during 2002 to be the Chairman of the U.S. Securities and Exchange Commission. William Donaldson did take up some concerns of international investments, and international terror in a complex way that intervened with some upper levels of management officials at Quest Communications Corporation. Upon the observation of some people and businesses (c/o Quest Communication Corp) various transaction issues, occasionally where considered as activities of an illegal hostile corporate take-over, and this is where the small investor is in it for the financial ride, and capital gains. The laws within the U.S. Constitution becomes very important when it applies to the good, and more so bad of foreign, and occasional domestic investors. This vitally includes certain business owners that do things against American's, and their "businesses or even employment opportunities that might be in the capacity of U.S. Anti-Trust law violations. WorldCom was even more so considered a U.S. Anti-Trust law violator which included certain buyout transactions. A real consideration of facts is that the observation of a "Junk Bond" market was becoming out of control for the bad values of business in America "such as destructive greed", and eliminating the productive growth of a small business or company.

Considering the United States financial markets, and the markets for computer service providers of information technology with "the Junk Bond" financial market concept of business during the 1990s was no stranger for new heavy market activity. America Online Company (AOL) with their CEO Steve Case operating as an internet web-site information provider, and shopping communication (.com) business was one of hundreds of businesses that went public during the 1990s. This communication, and internet business market expansion was not loss or underestimated. These company's and businesses offered new ways to do certain things, and therefore they were recognized for the new potential resource of the internet with the valuable understanding that investors, and business owners could find great achievements. In the contrary this new market resource was followed by the 1990s "Junk Bond Market Craze" that became out of control within marketing financial issues that kept certain public companies from becoming long-term stable businesses. The America Online Company (AOL) established an initial public offering with a growing business of over 1 to 20 million internet subscribers before a recession hit the .COM internet and communication markets, and industry. This was a stunning blow for certain investors, and more so the internet business owners that put vast amounts of money in these business ventures.

Understanding the vast amount of internet company's including AOL this was a good, but cautious time for long-term capital growth throughout most American internet / communication businesses. The growth and liquidity that AOL established from 1995 to 1999 made their merger agreement with Time Warner Inc. something of a "1 in every 10,000 token" for corporate American transactions. These merger factors can be observed from the liquidity value of Time Warner Incorporated. Time Warner Inc. had over 25 subsidiary companies as it applies to when Time Life Inc. (Time Incorporated) bough-out, and or had merger agreements with *the Warner Brothers (*Inc and or Corp.) Company to become Time Warner Inc.

The format of diversified corporations in America (c/o the 1990s and 2000s decades) have had a consolidation of good, and bad years of business results. Within these economic, and financial results a vital subject of decision making, and productive business programs where misguided by products, and the factual goal by most lawful professionals, business owners, and investors. This includes the understanding to achieve the highest, and most productive levels of business. Within what some individual investors (small, and large) look for is the consideration of earning money, and occasionally the brokers that they can earn investment income or money from within various publicly traded investment's, and companies.

One value of difference exist also when these investments are partly observed within the companies that are considered up for sale. Another part of this merger / buyout concern includes when a company has lower than expected prices within the stock market PE (price earnings ratios) listing of public company earnings. Considering this, outside business help within decisions is slightly irrelevant and occasionally unproductive especially if the original good of a business plan is not considered, or amended properly. Now the American investment community, with citizen investors, and business people have observed severe market difficulties, and complications within their involvement of investments, and the American economy. Considering themselves in corporate transactions that are considerably complex without a logical bottom, and even the top level of factors within business improvements, some corporate managements are failing. These are formal concerns, and economic worries within some publicly traded company issues becoming a true value of disaster.

Within the business resources of energy, and oil market issues of considered factors the good, and bad contingent liability business issues of corporation's such as British Petroleum Company, and more so Exxon Corporation has maintained some important participation in the financial markets, and the oil industry. These important factors within business markets of America where tested contingently when the Exxon Corporation reorganized their business format, and system of liabilities after an expensive accident that their company was held liable for. The liability of British Petroleum consisted of large amounts of employees, contractors, and even shareholders that sometimes take too many important details for granted. Understanding more so the Exxon Corporation whom also has subcontractors, this was observed different within the few corporations that bought into billions of dollars of investment issues with concerned liabilities. Considering these objectives the American base of industrial process businesses must reconstruct it's levels of safe, and responsible technical operating procedures.

Some corporate merged assets, and liabilities where reconsolidated, with certain issues of cost ranging into the hundreds of millions of dollars (c/o Exxon Corp. liquidity) where effected from prior objectives of good business decisions. This was achieved with market transactions, certain merger agreements involving Exxon Corporation which followed certain U.S. government regulation, and keeping investors, and employees focused. Even other American investors as good citizens including government should be concerned occasionally about the consistent resource of whom did other problem infested (c/o Enron & WorldCom) corporation's make rich, and wealthy. This is the concentration of wealth that should be used for the good of society, and not the bad! This is the National Security, and Securities & Exchange "contingent liability" effect, and concern besides what problems some businesses, and certain market's endured concerning the Exxon Corporation and the exception of a few other large corporations.

The Exxon Corporation (during 1989, and 1990) was factored with a huge liability factored accident, and condition of negligence when the Exxon Valdez oil tanker spilled 11 million gallons of oil into the Gulf of Alaska coastal waters. This environmental disaster, and accident perpetuated the killing of birds, and certain fish wildlife. During this accident it also caused heavy concentrations of severely oil contaminated sea waters. The Exxon Corporation spent tens of millions of dollars on the "cleanup", and the rescue of surviving sea life animals. Therefore years later during the early to mid-1990s they needed additional money, and helpful asset liquidity within business. This was occasionally the help and logical discipline of some mergers, and certain corporate work requirements. It is important to observe, and remember that the Exxon Corporation understood the serious nature of the Alaska oil spill disaster from the start. Therefore by taking control of the problem at the start in all phases, 10 to 15 years later the Exxon Oil Company's earnings have increased beneficially to the top of the corporate business list "financially" with likes, & dislikes, but as a very productive business operation. This is where the (Exxon Corp. & Mobil Corp.) ExxonMobil Corporation was a merger of possible good with logical business creation factors.

Next, and formally we have what was discussed throughout America without business logic of creating business with merger acquisition activity to become the largest company's (c/o various products) in the world. The concept of creating a business; not managing or building a large productive business is a discrepancy, which was similar to the problems of Enron, WorldCom, and a few other small, and large businesses. This also includes the merger's that are questionable as larger business expansions (c/o control of corporate stock) that where considered, and understood. Upon this expansion of corporate American merger's these factors happened within issues observed within the way (ISG) International Steel Group & Mittal Steel Corporation was started, and accumulated American assets.

The (ISG) Mittal Steel Corporation with Lakshmi Mittal was started after a vast amount of fatal steel plant explosions, and accidents that occurred in Northwest Indiana. Before this ISG was part of the brief ownership by Wilber Ross whom did not seem to want to take the steel industry serious, and then sold most of his major controlling amount of stock. This was also consolidated from a debated issue about foreign steel competition becoming a business threat to the American consolidation of steel manufacturing companies. These issues including the foreign management control of American corporations that sometimes include the bad legal issues of the United States Anti-Trust laws are a discrepancy of various United States Constitutional values. Considering other conflicts that where of procrastinated issues of contempt within the state, and federal courts, and this has been, and was part of a factual problem that included certain United States National Security concerns after the purchase by Lakshmi Mittal. This factored discretionary business conditions, U.S. government security measures, and American investment issues from unfulfilled government duties to recognize certain valued secured disciplines for the American general public. The issued facts with American small, and large investors (not foreign investors) have been also a deterrent of U.S. Anti-Trust law legal subjects. Within these concerned conditions of business, and more so government the format of mergers upon which where the balance of the American people and laws are to be considered upon logical enforcement. This has caused issues of concern that the courts may have had a solution for, if they had worked, and applied certain activities to the U.S. Constitutional environment of American industry.

The concept of business that consist of conflicting merger issues upon agreements that WorldCom Corporation was active in had discretionary values, and this level of activity should have been regulated by the United States Department of Justice's Anti-Trust division. Understanding this becomes very important due to monopoly restraint laws, and true values of competitive indifference which at that time affected some smaller businesses. Also the legal format and laws within the United States Public Utility Company Holding Act as it may apply to the money that the employees have invested in as a public utility service company was factored with corporate manipulation. These levels of manipulation are an endless loop crisis that became part of foreign business people taking control of a vast amount of American businesses that was interconnected to these large business failures. This was a violation within WorldCom's Anti-Trust law responsibilities considering other regulatory duties for the applicable liabilities within the Federal Communication Commission (Act) rules, and regulated laws concerning other businesses.

What has happened here with "Bernie Ebbers, and the IDB WorldCom Corporation", is similar to other businesses that forgot, and ignored the legal fact that a communication sectored company is not an investment brokerage firm. The company was started during the years of 1983, and 1984 in the state of Mississippi, and during some accumulated growth during the 1990s which also included name changes, and certain merger (buy-out) acquisitions of numerous communication company's, a certain level of greed, and control seem to be the goal. WorldCom is one of the corporate factors that outlined why the Junk Bond market was severely out of control. This was factual with WorldCom because they pursued over 40 to 60 acquisitions, and spending over $60 billion dollars between 1991, to 1997 which included a purchasing stake in MCI Communication Corporation.

Between the years of 1997 and 1999 WorldCom Corporation was involved in 2 or 3 merger's that seemed to have a consolidated value of $37 billion dollars, and $115 billion dollars. These WorldCom merger / buyout issued transactions where consolidated throughout various American domestic markets, and some European markets of business. Bernie Ebbers, and others including Scott Sullivan a WorldCom financial officer of the company found themselves with more than $14 billion dollars of debt. Understanding this, the conditional problems of money (cash holding, & market liquidity) became evident with the layoff of employees, and therefore they lacked productive liability's within business service provisions.

Some WorldCom business service provisions were being provided, but also with the unsatisfied discipline of work place liabilities, various employees loss most all hopeful ambition in the company. These problems consisted of a vast amount of concern for employee's losing everything that they had invested in the company over the years. Observing the United States Public Utility Company Holding Act regulated law issues, WorldCom Corporation like other public utility monopolies had a responsibility to 10s of thousands of employees, the corporate officials, and their customers, but then the business "severely" failed. The productive level of services with bad management consisted of a business that was within a corporate citizenship duty to maintain trustworthy liabilities to its customers, and the American society of business, and government. Considering the bad out-weighed the good they suffered within bad uncontrollable financial decision making, and issues of fraud. This was also observed in the factual display of the stock market price of the company. These conditions completely indicated failure just before the company filed for bankruptcy concerning this economic loss, and failure of asset liquidity, and liability.

The rules, and regulations of the United States Securities and Exchange Commission has a duty, and jurisdiction within government to enforce the laws of the securities and exchange markets, and investment banking. This applies to all small, and large investors including those as American business owners that are committed to a product or services with values lawfully, but are how they are looking to earn investment interest on their extra money. These duty's to enforce lawful regulation is also to observe certain unlawful activity that may be unfair to those people occasionally with less money, and business liquidity including assets. This includes when a business is not an "Investment Bank" to guide, and enforce "the United States Constitution, and laws" accordingly to any financial brokerage activity as it applies to the U.S. security and exchange investment market rules, and laws.

Another unfulfilled issue was the legal foundation enforced by the United States Anti-Trust laws, and certain vital laws under the Constitution of the United States that where ignored, and deprived to certain citizens, and business owners. Understanding this consolidation of events, and business failures within the communication, and telecommunication business sectors concerning their liabilities, thousands of employees loss assets, and then were factored with financial problems. Within the financial decisions of the WorldCom Corporation, and their merger concerning business issues of Anti-Trust laws of lawful competitive business concerns, this was only slightly in question by the United States Department of Justice's Anti-Trust Division officials. The United States federal government regulatory duties are vital factors considering these business, and bank transactions. This jurisdiction of legal concerns also consisted of certain small victimized American investors, people, and businesses considering the United States Constitutional laws, and the United States Anti-Trust laws which were not in their most formal investment conditions of resource. This was factual even more so when the business interest or concern to expand became complacent.

Both Enron Corp, and WorldCom Corp have several transactions that they pursued, and then ignored the facts within the most important liabilities of American specifications, codes, and standards that apply to certain market monopolies. This was the lawful concern that applies to different and diversified businesses within these companies working with monopoly status in the public utility sectors of industry to serve massive amounts of people residentially, and commercially. Observing the Enron Corporation this was a company with a valuable background in the "transmission and distribution" of electricity, and more so gas as the former Houston Natural Gas Company. This is where their ability to leverage asset liquidity came from to purchase others company's.

Enron Corporation was considered a very innovated company, and maybe too innovated. Besides how Enron Corp used, and involved themselves in a few large corporate (c/o the U.S. SEC market) mergers with the format of public utilities, energy trading, and some communication systems on a domestic, and international market, the "American society suffered". These including subsidiary company's may have served foreign issues of business and investors better than American concerns, and citizen constituents. Therefore the vast amount of billions of dollars that these company's controlled individually including stocks, and or bonds during 1995, to 2000 was not an (American) product, and service liability value within logical business liquidity, and stable earnings.

The Enron Corporation (c/o the Houston Natural Gas Co. & Portland GE) in Houston, Texas during 1999 had around 21,000 employees. Observing certain conflicting issues including innovated deal making energy trades, the Enron Corporation had, and was started with leveraged accounts, and margin accounts with cash holdings. This compounded resource of cash holdings then suffered accounting irregularities between Enron officials, and the Chicago accounting firm of Arthur Andersen Accounting. Large utility companies, and businesses such as the consulting engineers in certain large cities including a format of liability had part of this responsibility to support good public utilities, and business procedures, but various problems became complex. This also consisted of bank transactions, and accounting due to the many phases of engineering, construction, and maintenance, upon which they have a duty to provide payment disciplines with logical values of efficiency. This professional format of business conditions is factual to the public utility markets, which becomes vital on a "day by day" base annually. When Enron Corp became a heavily traded public (c/o energy & utilities) company, American "Engineering Professionals" suffered throughout this American public utility market. Considering WorldCom Corp, and Enron Corp. the concept of privately held company's working in this utility market sector of businesses consisted of a vast amount of different professional, and nonprofessional liabilities. This concept of professionalism included some occupations which where misguided from most American professional values that are vital, and applicable to responsible business. Therefore both of these corporations could not stabilize these so called innovated business procedures within market operations.

Besides the many certified public accountants, professional engineers, and even those business professionals that are licensed, or non-licensed financial workers, and brokers, the Enron Corporation suffered with these professionals, and illogical utility market business expansions. The Enron Corporation seemed to not have much concern for the American investor, and then expanded into different states, and foreign markets of certain countries. Therefore this ignored the financial disciplines that are important from the top, and bottom of companies that provides natural gas, and electricity services to most large, and small American metropolitan areas. This includes the issued understanding occasionally of what the public utility market in another country consist of including government regulation. These issues of American contingent liability base factors of market liquidity, is complex with various predictions for most residential, and commercial customers. Therefore any slight problems including weather related issues of nature consist of contingent liabilities of caution. Then this becomes a vital business, and personal issue of awareness observing that this is financially a part of those public utility matters without heavy, or discretionary borrowing from the bank, especially considering there is duties of liability that apply.

Enron Corporation, like most corporations, and businesses including the Exxon Corporation, and even the General Electric Corporation have, or had an open line of creditable lending business agreements with certain banking establishment's. This is the line of business credit within certain banking establishments, and the outline of business with banks, and investment banks which become a very serious factor. This logic to hold solid ground on economics, and professionalism is the format of discipline within business decisions. The multiple activity within what is considered as a communication company, and an energy trading company seemed to develop many types of business constituents, and transactions that occasionally looked good. Contrary to this factor a vital issue in these companies is how they manage, and provide a massive concentration of market liquidity. To understand Enron Corporation, and the factors of market liquidity, their investments, and investor's outside of the company consisted of a few businesses with resources of expandable liquidity.

American investments have a vast amount of objectives that are pursued in various lawful ways to earn money on what investments may consist of. A young, and more so older person's consolidation as outside investors manage their asset liquidity matters that are found in such markets like real estate, public utilities, renovation of properties within houses, and or apartments. This also includes some small business investments to increase value within future business opportunities of growth. Theoretically some valued investments in real estate have maturing obligations that if they are meet properly, certain business, and resident discounts can occur. Also within real estate concerning other issues of equity these are financial benefit rewards from good credit ratings. One vital definition of liquidity observing the financial markets is that it is outlined as; the characteristic of a security, or commodity with enough unites outstanding to allow large transactions without a substantial drop in price. Second, it can be a stock, bond, or commodity that has a great amount of shares outstanding, and therefore this means liquidity! Institutional investors are to seek out liquid investments so that their trading activity will not influence the market price factors. The Enron Corporate management officials and employees with investments failed to observe this issue of market liquidity, even with equitable "public utility, and monopoly" assets.

The Enron Corporation and even WorldCom Corporation did not have the ability with market liquidity of an individual, or company to convert assets into cash, or cash equivalents without suffering financial, and other business duty significant losses. Upon this relevant understanding the people, businesses, corporations, and occasionally government consist of issues to overcome the negative, and positive market transaction liquidity factors of the American society of businesses, and most financial markets. This is most times pursued with the best, and or most logical people, and professionals productively in business, and society. The state of California acquired state budget problems from this and other matters, and I've even seen it occasionally get bad in the state of Illinois. Contrary to the overall economics of these state government issues, California was hit quite hard within a 2001 possible energy crisis, claiming that Enron Corporation gouged California customers, and clients. The effect of this problem occurred in the western states of the U.S. during the California 2000, and 2001 crisis on energy which they suffered a severe amount of electrical blackouts with these market conflicts. Surly most logical people understand that this was fairly different from the 1973 Energy Crisis, and Oil Embargo, but one thing is for sure, and that is in all services (c/o even street light energy) "rarely is anything free". Therefore most all utility price's and markets have liabilities, and business liquidity responsibilities including various applicable U.S. Anti-Trust laws. This becomes important observing that all people involved in these business transactions including various individual state governments, and the federal government with some others must pursue lawful, and productive compliance.

Even as we observe other companies that have or had market liquidity such as Exxon Corporation, the Continental Illinois Bank of Chicago, and some factors of Harris Bank of Chicago, these businesses suffered due to high conflicting rates of liability. Considering the "different" liability of Exxon Corporation with a massive oil spill that generated harsh criticism, this problem fluctuated bad conditions of contingent equity, and liquidity that includes some conflicts observed within bank lending. From these various business disasters of a contingent crisis of liability, business disciplines within management are vital. Both businesses within Exxon Corporation, and Harris Bank recovered, contrary to the collapse of Continental Illinois Bank. This means various businesses including Exxon Corporation, and Harris Bank where able to recover liquidity values, and disciplines without too much long-term damage. Considering this, the years that they created profitable business earnings, and market share could be reestablished. There are hundreds of stories that include small, large, public, and private businesses that understood these issues within these complex times of business, and effort. Otherwise things possibly may get bad in business, and society upon which this therefore consisted of a logical amount of lawful subjects, and goals that must be recognized, and achieved.

With the understanding of company's such as the ExxonMobil Corporation, and even more so the United Airlines Corporation that suffered after the (9-11 Report) terrorist attacks, most businesses, and the American society has additional things, and issues that cause, or prevent markets, and people to react. ExxonMobil Corporation's losses where fractional, but United Airlines had to file bankruptcy a few years after September 11, 2001. The liabilities of financial brokers, making excessively large amounts of money, and earnings illegally (c/o lawful practices) in the financial markets becomes an issue that is reacted on also. The 9-11 terrorist attacks where reacted on from the American people in the United States that had second thoughts about regular travel on airplanes, and even occasionally with the use or purchase of cars, and other vehicles. Another conflicting market reaction was the enormous amount of money within stock options sold, and exercised by a vast amount of Middle Eastern investors in American companies, and markets after these attacks. Understanding this concern there has been individuals, and more so businesses to make hundreds of millions of dollars from the financial markets in a year. This occasionally is the effect of more than a small productive companies earning capacity with serious workable duties, and responsibilities to achieve progress.

The American society has also witnessed, and observed a vast amount of oil, and chemical spills, or "soil, and water contamination" issues within waterways (c/o large company's) that killed fish, different commodities including food, and damage to the American society. Large and small American businesses observe these worry's which includes how they manage their values of future liquidity. Considering these activities within bad business issues, the liability of all resources of society becomes a concern. These are even factors more so that consist of small company's making the effort to go public, and then "the question" is has the underwriting process of financial agreements within productive business been lawfully fair? This becomes the consideration of facts when a small or large company receives investment dollars, and the use of this form of liquidity makes businesses and other issues slightly complex. Understanding this within market opportunities to share the financial underwriting firms commitment which can cause harm to the financial investment process, these businesses must continue to prove their ability to do better, and be productively workable. Therefore the business risk and condition of reward even with damage to the American society has an equation not just in corporate mergers, but also within the American format of business decisions, and markets. These become relevant concerns that need lawful enforcement, and improvements applicable to the U.S. Constitutional laws, and other laws that are valuable to manage all resources of society

A terrorist attack (c/o 2001) made the American people worried for a while about traveling, and how to address the good, and more so bad issues of foreign relations. Just as the U.S. government and the President Bush Administration along with the Congress established the office of Homeland Security with the appointment of Tom Ridge after September 11, 2001 and then the government had an extra duty to relieve these worries. We must also include the changing times that "the American and Iraq" war is providing with diversified issues of important national security conditions with opinions and the disciplines of professional or business markets. This U.S. National Security issue vitally includes even some American collage-students, and even international student exchange conditions that America offers within college, and university studies. Also this could vitally include the effects of global business versus American businesses, and its effect on the people, and even government tax revenue throughout the United States. Therefore how we protect, and defend our American liabilities, markets, businesses, schools, and government upon other social values is with a factor of dignity, and commitment to serve, and respect the American society. These factors are lawfully based on what we give, receive, and hold as a nation of human decency, and work ethics. In addition this also is part of capitalism within what we understand to work for, and earn to provide a good life in the American society.

The format of what has been described in this chapter relates to the different people, and the effort they make to secure a business operation that is a public, or private corporation with good, and bad issues of successful outcomes. There is four people that come to my attention, and that is Jack Welch (former CEO) of General Electric Corporation, T-Boone Pickens of BP-America (c/o Mesa Petroleum), Reginald Lewis (Wall Street Buy-Out Lawyer) the former Chairman of Beatrice International, and John Johnson the founder of Johnson Publishing Co. with Ebony magazine. These individual business people have stood strong on their belief's within decision making, and logical values that could produce long-term prosperous business. Upon the fact that there are other vital American business people along with these American people throughout business whom have factored hard work, and earnings which most times their activity includes more likes, then dislikes from the American society. As for other younger people going into business at these levels have concern, the times have gotten worse, and more complex with businesses throughout America that must prevail with productive people, and resources.

Jack Welch took General Electric Corporation from $12 billion dollars in market value in 1981 to over $280 billion dollars in market value by 2002-2003. This was done at General Electric Corporation with a majority of good products, services, and marketable investments that included leveraged merger / buyout activity upon which most GE subsidiary businesses became profitable. T Boone Pickens started Mesa Petroleum during the 1950s & 60s with $2,500.00, and by the 1990s the Mesa Petroleum Company had a market value of over $2 billion dollars with units trading on the American Stock Exchange. The Mesa Petroleum Company was established in the state of Texas, and has operated throughout Texas, Oklahoma, and various other oil producing states in America. His format of business penetrated the oil industry, and a few other markets throughout some other countries which includes some capacity of being a corporate raider with various leveraged merger / buyout acquisitions throughout America. In addition T-Boone Pickens pursued a format of business within effort of applicable growth in an oil company, and penetrated the American oil industry which included other markets throughout various other countries. The concept of Mesa Petroleum, and T-Boone Pickens also had involvement in certain capacities of American off-shore oil drilling, and production concerns which became conflicting, but profitable.

Reginald Lewis was a New York Wall Street lawyer that was raised in one of the poor black communities of Baltimore, Maryland. During the years of 1984, and 1985 he consolidated a buyout of Beatrice International "Food" Company for $985 million dollars. This was a leveraged buyout that was formatted from a company he started in 1983 called the TLC Group upon where he worked thru certain leveraged buyout activities that earned him, and his family $50 million dollars in certain profitable business deals. Besides a lawyers salary he achieved this starting with $1 million dollars in equity. Some professionals, and government officials would say his occasional deal making, and management transactions of asset funds would be illegal if the company became insolvent. The company, and Reginald Lewis held too much complicated market liquidity from unsecured investments, and his ownership stake within cash holdings had a complex time expanding. This made Beatrice International with the Chairman Reginald Lewis a complex or questionable publicly traded company, and therefore during his hard work, his health gave out with him passing away from a heart attack. During the effort to take the company public with an Initial Public Offering consisting of a complicated group of known, and some unknown investors, this becomes an unknown market, and business of managing stable liquidity until result's are evident.

The late John Johnson of Chicago, and the private company that he started Johnson Publishing Company consist of 2 popular magazines, and various other publication's that are written about black Americans. John Johnson and Johnson's Publishing Company had positive involvement with writing about an assortment of issues that have good, and bad effects on America, and it's black communities. Ebony, Ebony Jr., and Jet magazines with Johnson's Publishing Company have been around in circulation for over 40 years approaching the millennium years of 2000. These magazine publishing products have been distributed in almost all places throughout the United States, and some parts of the world. This private company grew from a small operation on the south side of Chicago to establish great wealth, and productive business activities in Chicago, and the United States. The Johnson's publishing company held stable, and logical advancements of growth, and wealth as a privately held company with good concerns of liability. These are the public, private, and productive issues of certain investments in America that include other complex, and resourceful markets.

The Expansion And Failures of Business
(5)

CHAPTER FIVE
(5)

The United States Library of Congress

The Expansion And Failures of Business
(5)

The history and innovation of business, and corporations in America has consisted of many ways, and years of leveled business financial growth, and prosperous expansions into different markets. These are valued issues upon which also occasionally includes certain conditions of failure. This formal concern for American business people and citizens are valued with good, bad, and complex issues of prosperity. In addition this is valued within the many subjects of decision making, and the marketable conditions of the American general public. Within the concept of expansions, and failures observing businesses that have created asset gains, and occasional losses within certain business matters this process must be controlled lawfully in all possible, and productive ways. A consolidated resource in this format of continued business, and market decisions is the process of business expansions that consist of working professionally in a productive capacity to avoid failure. Company's such as Esmark, Beatrice Food International, General Mills Corporation, PepsiCo Incorporated, and Coca Cola Company have expanded for decades. Other Corporation's such as Ford Motor Company, General Motors Corporation, General Electric Corporation, and a vast amount of others have provided innovated levels of expansion with their markets of concern.

The logic of business expansion within the progress of smaller businesses in America is a factual concern within various important market, and lawful business challenges. These challenges within expansion also consist of a verity of occasional complex decisions made easy. This process of expansion challenges is perceptional with some working values of caution. The American small business concept of determination includes various laws which is an observation of logical factors that are used in this vital resource of business awareness, and planning in our American society. With most small, and ambitious business owner's the government has state and federal "Anti-Trust laws, and other regulated issues that the American small business owners can maintain for a successful operating level of discipline. At some point, and time various businesses may become logical competitors, and this logic is a responsible outlook with the laws of the American system of government. Considering this decade within the years of 2000, the American society of business will likely continue to consist of these types of business activity's with governed liabilities, and market rates of a good, and bad capacity.

Over the last 100 years American businesses have achieved good market gains, and appropriate capital gains from certain products, and services becoming innovated. The gains, and appreciation that innovation provides is within the format of complying with the laws, workable commitments, and the United States Constitutional disciplines of society with tranquility, that appropriates business prosperity. Most people see this in many different ways politically, but government facts always apply, just like the conditional format of responsibilities that a business owner has to apply with their concerns of business discipline. This is also found in corporations that maintain productive resources within their employees. Most business constituents (c/o good networking) are developed in this way, and that keeps society, and business prosperous, upon living life in a lawful way. These become some of the most important levels of determination factors within the success, or failure of a business.

There is, and has been many different markets, and business issues that appropriate prosperity with earning income, and business liquidity of an expanding capacity. These conditions consist of a strong marketing level of supply, and demand in most all business communities of America. Within the consideration of the supply, and demand levels for products, and services of the American society, this factor has achieved great levels of prosperity with the awareness of good earnings, more so then bad financial, and economic outcomes which can occur. Throughout the years, certain businesses have established a market level of liability that provides them growth, and increased assets under their secured levels of management. This is vitally observant in massive manufacturing facilities where various amounts of products that are manufactured every year increases to keep up with the proper levels of demand. For most American businesses, and corporations the increase in products is a continuous observation of how levels of inventory, product storage resources, and distribution is managed during most quarterly issues of evaluation. The American automobile industry, certain major appliance manufactures, and others are sometimes observed with these inventory issues due to market demands with vital issues, and economics.

Issues of inventory over the years of the 1970's, and 1980's have provided an offering of enormous amounts of effort by businesses to manage their marketable manufactured products. This is the format of how important it is to equate the consolidated assets of manageable inventory for a business to appropriate supply, and demand. Homes, cars, major appliances, various chemicals, and other types of products require the proper procedures with facilities including equipment to manage inventory. These management, and inventory conditions also has factored the good, and bad issues of how some company's evaluated years of business within establishing progress that is managed, and maintained with careful, and logical decisions.

During the late 1970s, and early 1980s the most complicated issues were tax, and accounting disciplines to manage multiple business locations where the regional district tax on the storage of products, and equipment had struck a business tax inventory debate. This business concern made complicated issues within different government tax rates (c/o adjustability and deductions) having an important cost to observe, and evaluate. Considering these taxes some businesses had to observe, and outline this as unfair upon surviving in business. These tax, and accounting issues with the full consideration of inventory are important to the businesses that must comply with observing these duties, and stay competitive. An example of businesses that survived with determination, and advancements could be seen between PepsiCo Incorporated, and Coca Cola Company within canning, bottling, and distribution. They both also consist of multiple refreshment flavored drinks with various facilities and locations for supply, and demand throughout the United States, and internationally. There biggest expansion was going from one flavor of drinks to multiple amounts of flavored drinks with production disciplines domestically, and internationally.

Another process within distribution, and demand factors are found between Apple Computer Corporation, and Microsoft Corporation having competitive ambition for various computer products, and shipping processes throughout America, and various parts of the world. Observing smaller businesses that have a small fraction of a market share this caused occasional debates between businesses, and or corporations about the good, or bad of the American system of government. Therefore with taxable products and distribution resources, this is how economic planning consist of values which becomes better factors within business, and personal sacrifices. Contrary to indifferences, the increase in inventory, and other business items can be observed as these businesses also create a tax revenue base in the American system of government that is important.

Managing business issues of inventory have been true values with the concerned discipline, and important earning liquidity values within the process, and procedures of most all American food companies, and farming. Observing most agriculture, and farming issues for the business wholesale and retail disciplines, this process is considered in their food commodity inventories with careful disciplines of consideration apart from the important tax, and business matters that apply. This is found in businesses such as General Mills Corporation, Beatrice Foods International, and certain other food processing businesses. Their food products throughout the industry, and government has a liability too stay fresh as a safe product thru the distribution processes to the general public. Within the jurisdiction, and duties of the United States Department of Agriculture, the markets of leading product groups in America are cereal grains, root crops, fruits and vegetables, milk, oil bearing crops, fish, and meat. This is also applicable to the means of food from various 'live-stock extracted animal parts, various sea life extracted food parts, and all other produce grown, raised, and retrieved within the American system of farming. These food products including occasional medicine are regulated by the U.S. Food and Drug Administration (FDA) that evaluates certain items for sale, and then more so food must be held within the United States Department of Agriculture's (USDA) standard of approved quality.

Certain FDA approved medicines are also discovered in certain ocean waters consisting of sea life, and plants that require these special disciplines within obtaining certain ocean water sea life species, and conditional plants. These are plants, and sea life which also require various special or applied conditions of evaluation to produce various ingredients. Medicines are made from agriculture farming products more so, but this becomes more of a combined, and or occasionally separated duty observed by both the Food and Drug Administration, and the U.S. Department of Agriculture's process of review, and inspections. Considering these business commodities which are understood by the United States government, and various businesses they will apply research, and testing for the safety, and effectiveness of these sectored products. These safe, and effective products of "food, beverages, internal medicine" and other internal use products for animals, and especially humans also by law consist of labeled contents, ingredients, and logical instructive use directions. This market, and commodity issue within years has expanded. Therefore the people including the U.S. government, upon whom makes an effort to maintain a logical format of regulated disciplines that people, and business live with lawfully, is observed with arbitrational, and appropriate relevance.

Observing productive business matters various other important issues within the American markets applicable to agriculture include values of farm production, sales of cotton, most all tobacco items, and other non-durable commodities, and items. These are to be considered in the right format of business, and the laws that keep American values safe with reasonable understanding of the American society. This also occasionally includes soda pop, and alcoholic beverages. Cotton, and tobacco are byproducts in the textile, and smoking industry, and sector of products in the American markets that consist of lawful concerns for their product factors of liability. Both alcoholic beverages, and tobacco smoking products consist of regulatory age requirements within legal statue conditions. This occasionally gets a little different from various non-alcoholic beverages which have expanded like other sectors of business to the extent of various safety values that are appropriately considered. The textile, and cotton format of industry goes a long way in marketing with all types of clothing's, bed linens, automobile interior, furniture, and a vast amount of other things. These are some of the agriculture marketing, and inventory issues that the United States government, and the American system of farming try to work together on. This was established thru state, and federal government concerns so that all values of protecting the farmer, and the general public are in lawful order.

Some farming legislature concerning markets, crop lands, and different commodities are dated back to the 1700s, and 1800s, and therefore even today (c/o 2000 to 2009) the new farming legislature is considered with the format of new farming procedures, and technology. Occasionally, business conditions between agriculture, most grocery store chain's, and even to the extent of auto manufacturing with sales issues including inventory, are the structure of retail business operating procedures. These also become vital disciplines to business management duties which has a variety of responsibilities. This is a format of balance concerning the process within logic of observing government concerns to provide lawful values in the American general public. This includes the regulatory condition of the individual state governments that consist of many departments, and types of taxable concerns to appropriate the people, and business values of society. One of many corporations that recognized this issue of government taxes, and court matters within large amounts of inventory include certain textile, and steel products is the Chrysler automobile corporation. The Chrysler Corporation and a few others had to pursue different business concerns similar to the food industry, and agriculture product inventories that intervened with their profitable earnings. This also was a problem within their vehicle finance issues within this concentration of American business sector's which is applicable to thousands of auto dealers. An inventory issue of serious concern was observed when Chrysler Corp encountered trouble within the sale of their automobile products that slipped to low levels during the 1970s. This increased a factor and supply of inventory that was massive, and out dated. When a corporation has large amounts of outdated inventory that the business's, and corporation's cannot sale, the business, and corporation suffers.

Chrysler Corporation, General Electric Corporation, some "shoes, and clothing" store corporations and others have had to endure the inventory factor of good, and bad product sale's with the evaluation of what, and how to liquidate without too big of a cost factor. Understanding obsolete inventory within businesses, and corporations that have suffered with how to control leftover inventory such as when Chrysler Corporation could not sale certain cars fast enough, the format of things lingered into the liquidity concerns of bankruptcy. This was the concern of how to consolidate the massive inventory of the Chrysler Corporation that had an effect on other businesses, and government. This problem went as far as the United States Bankruptcy Court's, and the Chrysler Corporations findings of a troubled business plan. These troubled times also caused a problem that the corporation had concerning inventory upon which the United States government could not easily compensate payment of "too liquidate". Therefore when businesses expand, the integrity of inventory is a big factor within managing the large, or small business considerations of successful operating disciplines, and taxable earnings.

Within issues that factored certain good, and bad problems in business, the coordinated evaluation issue of inventory, and governed taxes expanding certain resources of business is not always a common factor to destroy businesses. Contrary to this working effort in business, occasionally certain levels of inventory became an important issue within productive business factors. Considering these business subjects that occasionally occur with problems, there are other issues, and markets that consist of managing complex inventory, and taxable concerns. These businesses that manufacture, and sale certain large ticket item's (c/o complex taxes & inventory) includes purchases occasionally from certain United States government contractors and other large corporations, and business. Certain U.S. government contractors such as within the General

Electric Corporation, and others have developed products especially manufactured, and prepared for the U.S. concept of research, and certain technical process conditions of procedures. Understanding these issues of business even with telephone companies like AT&T, and Comcast the better values of logic become the best disciplines observed as factual.

Technical process disciplines, and research was done for the conditional evaluations of agencies like the National Aeronautics Space Administration (NASA), and or the National Oceanic Atmospheric Administration (NOAA). It's products like the NASA Skylab Space Capsule equipment, and the Lunar-Rover where used in the orbit of outer space to land, and travel on the orbital conditions of the moon. In addition this consisted of certain NASA satellites, and more so solar panels with the understanding for the vital need of equipment to function with electrical power. These factors of equipment with large quantities of fuel helped improve landing exploration projects near, and or on the moon. Also throughout this process in the orbit of outer space these conditional provisions consisted of solar electrical power being generated with the appropriate distance from the sun. Another consideration of study is meteorology (c/o NOAA) that helps to predict catastrophic weather conditions that help save lives, and sometimes people's property. Within these American products, and scientific studies this expansion of helpful tools with procedures has provided disciplines of efficiency in the United States, and around the world.

Observing the U.S. government projects of the National Oceanic Atmospheric Administration, and the National Aeronautics Space Administration, these NASA and NOAA administrations have expanded in America with scientific principals and technology. The expansion, and technology has advanced with the expanded sense that the U.S. Spacecraft Shuttle and Shuttle Flight Program now lands the spacecraft on a airport runway coming from outer space.

This same U.S. Space Capsule procedure, and equipment changed from a process that would splash down in the ocean as the space journey, and mission had come to an end. These special products ordered, and developed by the United States government, and NASA with certain contractors required large amounts of additional parts as inventory. Considering the format of the Chrysler Corporation this also consisted of the manufacture of the United States Army jeeps, hummer military vehicles, and other vehicles such as the orbiter Luner-Rover. Navistar International Corp, and AM General (c/o GM) also has been a vital part of manufacturing these new truck Hummer, and the U.S. military vehicle Humvee diverse products for defense, and civilian use. Observing this, it seems that doing business with the United States government is very beneficial financially, but this also can develop a cast of cost over runs that consist of vital corrections with massive corporate evaluation processes.

Considering the observation from large government research and development projects, technological expansion also consisted of mass production manufacturing. A vast amount of parts for certain products that the United States Government (c/o NASA & NOAA) ordered, and paid for came from the General Electric Corporation, the Chrysler Corporation, Raytheon Corporation, and others. Most of the time these corporation's would manufacture, and develop large ticket government items, and parts that where eventually made just as well for the American general public to purchase, if it could be regulated with proper lawful use. These are corporations that have maintained certain levels of business progress, and the ups, and downs of market liquidity, and liabilities within large government contracts. Observing these products such as airplanes, tires, war ship vessels, and military tanks with parts for defense provided by Northrop-Grudman Corp., Boeing Corp. and the Goodyear Tire Corporation a concept of liabilities was maintained with established negotiated agreements. All of these corporations consist of large manufacturing equipment process disciplines that must be maintained with the highest levels of cost effectiveness, and stable market liquidity. This is part of their ability to advance levels of production within their business operations as United States government contractors. These are the company's that understand from "time to time" how to expand within their marketing of products, services, manufacturing, sales, and distribution.

It is clearly observant that most businesses, and corporations expand for the right reasons, and not wastefully (c/o economics) for any wrong reasons. These types of bad business decisions can cause financial losses, and issues of failure. Although during the 1990s the automobile industry started expanding as they have done for decades throughout the state of Michigan, and this process was an economic, and product advancement concern. Some of these new vehicle manufacturing facilities became part of a wasteful financial business expansion, but some progress was important with competitive factors. These near wasteful spending issues consisted of diversified opinions, and then some auto markets suffered with certain levels of "near" failure consequences. This almost was at the tune of failure for other major American corporations whom where involved with commitments to manage. Observing various American corporate franchise businesses the small, and large business effect was another vital concern as even automobile dealerships have had to be closed. This severely is where American born citizen factors of appropriate hard work, and various state and federal constitutional laws may have been part of the vital economics. From these expense factors of logic upon the cost, and lawful earning measures that where ignored, decisions had to be made to adjust earnings, and survival.

Between the Ford Motor Company, General Motors Corporation, and Saturn Corporation, the biggest financial losses where (c/o 2006) with the Ford Motor Company having estimated losses of $9 billion dollars, and buying out an estimated 70,000 employees.

The Saturn Corporation was established, and owned by the General Motors Corporation, and now due to the 2009 bad economy Saturn Corporation was put on a corporate auctioning block. Upon this factor of failure the Saturn automobile product line was a good, and very successful line of compact American cars. Therefore these became issues of a problem that all factors from a corporation's management must correct certain difficulties. This is vital within their long term market liability plans of business liquidity, production, and sales. Usually the American automobile industry most times has a tendency of knowing what's important to restructure too improve earnings within adjustments to bad economic, and production times within the American, and international markets.

Chrysler Corporation is the pivotal vehicle manufacturing business of American hard work disciplines. The people as employee's consolidated throughout management, and labor union constituents is the real work horse at Chrysler Corporation. Some of these factors have established this company as the most unpredictable due to its level of intellectual isolation, and sporadic values of hard work to establish interesting vehicle products. This on occasions gave Chrysler Corporation a set of logical values within certain business operations, and issues of expansion. It's not easy to call Chrysler a middle man (c/o maybe a conservative) company because GM, and Ford observe certain market diversions. This evaluation and concept of diversions consist of complex issues of expansion when profitable earnings are questionable. Considering these issues, and the factors that make Chrysler Corporation an interesting, but valued business, is how they expand, but also work to keep liabilities in productive order. Therefore they have had to work hard at it, upon the factual discipline from its workers, and production.

The format of expansions, failures, and liabilities in most small, and large businesses including some corporation's has become diversified, but similar. This is the observation within how the tire manufacturing industry, and the airplane manufacturing industry take in an evaluation on how many products they need to manufacture without a financial loss. Within the diversified format of certain company's such as food processing company's like General Mills Corporation whom expands or improves most of their manufacturing disciplines of products this is done to keep up with most lawful standards, and product demand. Another issue of good, and bad expansion concerns is the formal level of business production to distribute these products at a large, and small business capacity of grocery stores, and other business locations.

Every automobile manufacture needs tires made from companies like Goodyear Tire & Rubber Company, Uniroyal Inc., Firestone Tire & Rubber Company, and a few others. This therefore consist of the amount of tires manufactured (c/o GDP) which becomes important to compensate all types of car's, truck's, and other vehicles. This also applies to the tires that the Boeing Corp, and Raytheon Corp require for the various airplane's that they manufacture. Then we observe vehicle parts, and the food distribution process of factual markets, and inventory where this is pursued at a logical rate of supply, and demand for conditions of turnover rate quotas. This means that the wholesale and retail sales rates are pursued at logical amounts of supply, and demand within ordered quantities.

Considering the likeliness or necessity of the products, this evaluation stabilizes the marketable liability of most all diversified responsible products. This is also vitally true within the supply, and demand of parts for automobiles, trucks, airplanes, and even the tires these vehicles use, which became a market for vehicle parts, and or services that have different levels of demand. These are important items that are included within the safe, and responsible travel conditions that apply to the laws of maintenance, and liability of most transportation vehicle's. Most tire company's work to maintain this order of business operation's within liabilities, and product specifications for most types of small, or large auto repair centers, and the concept of truck, and airplane's hanger repair centers.

All American cities, towns, states, and the United States federal government observe, and enforce the vehicle specifications within tires, mirrors, windows, exhaust systems, and some other items as vitally important to safe, and resourceful travel. Over the decades this includes products established for the roadway safety laws throughout America, and some other countries. Considering this is a legal subject of fact for a vast amount of vehicle mechanical parts concerning these requirements that must apply to the American system of laws, all associated companies, and motorist are held liable. Observing the lawful liability of all types of vehicles, and this therefore means you have by-products such as windows, lights, brakes, mirrors, and other details including sometimes radios that lawfully must apply to certain issues of safety regulation. Also all of these additional, or original parts, and other manufactured parts from various different companies have legal specifications to compensate the products liability. These product liability, and safety codes of efficient operating conditions has consistently become a resourceful business and market sector responsibly. Appropriately, this is part of the company's product patent disciplines that factor a certain level of the company's liability protection. Therefore most of their product right's, and their concept of operating liabilities of existence for the product sales to the general public is factored so that all business conditions are maintained in logical order.

Most all products that certain corporations consist of within manufacturing have registered trade mark's, including patent right numbers. This is most times the specified identification number of a company or businesses group of products. Automobiles, televisions, and even computers that include the software that computers need to operate different computer programs of data have patent rights, and specified codes that outlines the products liability. Within the concept of computer software programs, and even the intervention of televisions or computer monitor screens, these are products with a logical format of liability, and compatibility. This important factor of liability, and compatibility within parts, programs, and services has expanded during the 1990s, and 2000 at rates that are good for certain company's, and most logical businesses, but this has created issues of unlawful oversight. Understanding the issues of oversight on new products, and undeveloped markets it sometimes takes years, and even a few product recalls before products improve or become adjusted to any, and all lawful use. Therefore it is common that the capacity of good, and bad issues of computer systems, and services apply to various conditions of liability. These liabilities are vital conditions in a legal capacity that needs to be regulated better with legal enforcement, and lawfully aggressive corrections. Some business professionals would almost compare enforcement to making it illegal to watch TV too much at work on a computer. Understanding this logic, the odds of productive employment activities are then within the format of better business discrepancies.

Considering, and understanding product, and service business issues of arbitrational factors, the computer, and software industry including internet service providers has observed massive expansions, and failures. Some people would say it's been a wild market, and concern within businesses that need or require enormous regulating duties from most all state, and U.S. federal government legislators. During the 1990s the concept of these internet businesses that are IBM, Microsoft, and Apple computer compatible have achieved large, small, and diversified business success, and earnings. Following these industry issues of computer, and internet arbitrational expanded services a vast amount of individuals, and businesses have engaged in obvious, and complex acts of fraud. These issues of fraud were pursued with peoples personal data information causing issues within the manipulation of certain peoples secured assets, privacy, and even procedures within purchases of certain items.

Arbitrary computer data services have reached the level of financial, and personal information security that is occasionally dangerous in America. The level of security has fallen to all-time lows with the expansion of "computer internet" service business concerns, and diversified activities. Some internet dating between men and woman couples went to the extent of violence, and negative conflicts during the course of people considering a sexual relationship. Another issue is the rate of older Americans that are victimized at the capacity of robbery or financial fraud. These are not good concerns for most business growth, and expansion issues that can have too much potential to cause hurt, and damages to the American society. This also exist to the extent that the American system of government must do their part, because if it is not regulated with better enforcement of the laws, the economy, national security, and other logical or law disciplines in America will fail. For now during the years of 2006, and 2007 vast amounts of people, and businesses are being prosecuted for certain diversified crimes with internet computer services, but sometimes regaining the money, or self-esteem is not as fair. This only slightly consisted of the recognized damages that are near critical financial liquidating capacity. Observing this sometimes includes even "fatally manipulated conditions of domestic terror, criminal intent, and or negligence".

Within the relevance of a computer internet service business that seems to produce more crime, and even advertise violence, and other unethical conduct, the American system of government during the first decade of 2000 has fallen behind without an outline of liability, and laws. Theoretically the factual problems consist of the vast amount of destructive things that people can maintain access to, and cause harm to others with. This subject concerning the values of support for destructive activities within what we would like to consider different from maintaining a moral, safe, and productive society has taken America backwards. This was clearly observed within some young people in America becoming not only just a problem within the psychology of violent video games, but a few bad occasions like the Collibine High School shooting massacre which was a conflict of promoting violent hate. Then the violent shooting attack (c/o terror) against students, and faculty at Virginia Tech University in 2007 was a disaster within the killing of over 25 people. The Virginia Tech attack was disastrous with conditions similar to mass hypnosis (but more so a lack of U.S. National Security) within bad foreign, and domestic ideals.

Each time certain violent attacks have happened these young people, and occasionally some older people have seem to be under a destructive influence. Also some issues within factors of international students, and conflicting activities have surrounded, and engaged themselves with certain internet use. Observing this they all had heavy involvement, and use of the internet that is a vital legislative issue of concern that has been discussed only briefly for governed legislature. This is an important factor within creating violent threats from video's that they engaged in before killing a vast amount of people, or causing failure to businesses, and society. Vitally this is a sad factor within issues of liability that is not being enforced by the United States Constitutional dignity of tranquility that has clearly became unrestricted free speech, and complex threats to the human rights of most American citizens. Therefore the businesses within website publishing, and distributing violence on film has instigated crime, and destruction at worrisome rates. This is a problem in America that is creating one of the worse computer tool, and operating concerns with a lack of lawful regulation that is disastrous. Considering these factors our American society has understood, or recognized these issues, and then the lawfully concerned level of criminal intent has reasons, and probable cause that consist of serve problems.

Upon how this market of computer operating conditions that exist, these crimes, and or negligence have occurred with sad factors of liability. Considering the format of businesses that must find consolidated corrections for the American society that has observed this vital problem "various" corrections, legislature, and enforcing the laws are vital. Within any logical state, and federal legislature of helpful procedures, and effort for most professional business people within our American society of the United States, this formal issue of factors can most times improve without massive failure. These failures have been outlined as bankruptcy, government cases of fraud, and other unlawful or unethical conditions of sex, crime, and or violence. Fraud, and these issued problems must be corrected by the American system of executive, legislative, and judicial procedures of government.

All these conditions within business considering the expansion of internet companies has not been completely full of business failures, and crime. There is a number of companies that have achieved proper business levels of success such as the Ebay Company, the Yahoo Company, the Amazon (.Com) Company which includes a vast amount of established businesses, and various products. These companies, that take orders, and advertise on the (.Com) internet is circulated to millions of people. In addition a vast amount of government web-sites consist of subjects that are occasionally helpful. Upon this consideration of markets, liabilities, and businesses in America these internet company's including ones like American On Line (AOL) have generated an enormous amount of money, and business market liquidity. Contrary to these factors it is also observant that these businesses just like others have had financial gains, and losses that must be managed, just like all conditions of lawful business in America. Therefore the American society has made progress with some internet businesses, and corporations that have found a successful way to achieve their business goals within operations. These are the productive and good factors that lawfully exist within various computer internet service providers to the American general public.

The expansion of business within the American commercial banking industry has fallen on hard times due to various junk bond market transactions, and issues of collateralized debt obligations from investment banks. When and during the late 1990s, and the early 2000s vast amounts of banks with large asset holdings of cash, pursued the purchase or merger of various small commercial banks. This lead to economic commitments that some of the larger commercial banks with investment subsidiaries could not compensate in the long term business process. These consolidated issues involved commercial bank lending that became insolvent due to a diversified resource of business economic difficulties. Therefore observing how banks expanded before suffering a crisis like Wachovia, and Countrywide their business plan was not of a real progressive business market discipline to serve their customers.

Considering all types of American investors that were hurt in the good, and then more so bad junk bond / merger market process Wachovia, and Countrywide banking institution's suffered non-traditional banking activity. Both of these commercial banking establishments purchased other smaller banks, and then they indulged in complex mortgage lending accounts throughout the United States that failed with expensive foreclosures. These mortgages that went into foreclosure consisted of investment items within "Mortgage Backed Securities". Observing the "Mortgage Backed Securities" factor these banks lacked local management disciplines of mortgage lending in a close proximity of their banking officials business office disciplines to be a productive bank. Bad loans within the process of default consist of expensive foreclosures, and this severely became too expensive to a bank's business operating budget. These are illogical problems between the American citizens, and government which includes the problems endured by the active or retired employees of Wachovia, Countrywide and the other smaller banks. Actually some smaller banks that where well managed seem to do better during these economic times of failure in America. This is factual because they expanded (c/o mergers and buyouts) with complex Junk Bond purchase agreements, and unlawful activity that they will dreadfully spend years trying to recover from.

These are, and will be some of the good "looking" (c/o productively true) business expansion issues of American business that more than likely consist of some good, and bad opinions with issues from the citizens, and government in the future years to come. It's not easy to predict the future, but all good businesses have an outline for their future business operations, and plans that consist of logical goals. Considering these things in our American society of business, these concerns become the most important factors of where market capitalism is achieved in the American system of market's, and business.

The People, Liabilities, And Business
(6)

CHAPTER SIX
(6)

The United States Library of Congress

The People, Liabilities, And Business
(6)

One of the most critical American issues of the last decade of the 1990s is the vast amount of people that have suffered damages within themselves, their families, friends, and some capacity of their livable assets. The consideration of livable assets, and liabilities in America for the last two decade's was, and is at the point that things should have improved, but in some cases we have found that to be slightly inaccurate, and difficult to consider as true. Upon this concerned observation with significant liabilities, even the businesses we trust have factored severe problems for ourselves, or certain people we may know. These become the decisions, and things of a very complicated format within standard of living issues, and the consideration of how the people, and businesses will establish a resource to get better. One of the vital answers is that the liability of people's health, and the values of life that they depend on for them living, working, and being productive has been threatened by social conflicts. Therefore the people's liability, and various concerns of business becomes vital to their conditional values of prosperity.

Upon any small levels of good, and bad decisions which people make mistakes that they can correct, and do better with, becomes our foundation for productive living. This is the value of American's to achieve certain factual goals of a U.S. Constitutional liability resource of capacity. Occasionally, even U.S. Constitutional Justice is vitally important to this liable process for the American people, and businesses to maintain standards of prosperity. Therefore, there is no productive liability in any person that consistently makes the proper levels of effort in the American society to work, and prosper to die, or suffer (c/o even finances) with destructive liabilities. These liability issues become the established values of prosperity considering (We the People) upon all citizens that make those every day efforts of decency to apply quality to most subjects of life in America.

A decade chronological observation of American people with tragedies of liability clearly compounded a vast amount of economic, and social problems during the 1990s, and the first conditional years of 2000. This is factual within the consideration that during the first Persian Gulf War, and the United States military buildup in the "Middle East" no solders, and or any people died in the intense conflict upon declaring a war to fight. This was the declaration of President George Z. Bush Sr., and his executive orders within U.S. Defense matters in the Persian Gulf. These where factual conditions during the United States Department of Defense military operation from 1989 to 1990 in a foreign land (c/o Iraq) upon which they held American hostages. Then during 1992 a "bomb and explosion" caused severe damage to certain parts of the underground parking garage below the street at the World Trade Center buildings in New York City causing six people to die from a terrorist plot. Also some parts of the upper levels of the facility where damaged in this explosion, but this was even more so a threat to the people, and liabilities of safety within the businesses in those office buildings.

Throughout the next five, to ten years following 1992 a vast amount of fatal manufacturing explosions occurred which caused a lack of discipline, and financial problems of liability to businesses, and various individuals including their families. This was a lack of discipline, and secured liability at these manufacturing (corporate) facilities where the equipment, and the people suffered in various way's. This vitally included people with injuries, and various fatalities, and this became another insured set-back for various businesses. An example within loss of liquidity, and liability occurred at a Lear Corporation facility in Northwest Indiana when a massive fire caused the plant to be shut down for two years. This becoming an increasing problem within various businesses their employee earnings, and levels of production where reduced tremendously. Considering these problems of liability including the September 11, 2001 terrorist attacks the American society was severely lacking governed, and business awareness of controlling liability resources. This goes along with additional U.S. National Security, and safety issues becoming the observed factual problem. Now the United States has factored financial losses, and fatalities that damaged the market of American businesses, and the future of certain places of employment.

Within the state of Indiana a concentration of violent crimes was rising, and factored a serious social problem. Contrary to these social conflicts in Northwest Indiana there was 3, or 4 major steel plant explosions that occurred within truly outlining another severe problem. The ignorance within violent crime is one thing, but a fatal explosion in a steel plant can be socially, and financially tremendous. In Northwest Indiana the magnitude of a fatal explosion at the Bata Steel Corporation that killed 3 people, and included many other people injured, is part of the diversion of fatal negligence, or can be factored as (inadmissible contingent) criminal intent. Upon admissible contingent factor's now this steel production facilities equipment was completely destroyed, and this includes with not to many other people to work in that part of the facility again for months, and years to come productively. This is one of many economic liabilities that totally destroyed a place of employment, and the business production facility to factor a severe social problem.

Due to what capacity of negligence within one, or two businesses or individuals including the Bata Steel Corporation, and the 1995 fatal explosion, the "plant", the "business" and employees suffered.

This was a multi-million dollar problem for the employee's, and concerned American citizens of Indiana that was factored in the steel industry of America. The steel production market issue within this steel mill facility, and the operating capacity of production including plant workers became a large loss to society. Therefore if the format of technology was a guarantee to improve liabilities within business production, a vital consideration to correct other problems lingered. This is a factual concern within the format that the management, and or labor unions or employees must be consistent with discipline for better, and more logical business conditions of support with all employment duties.

Observing government liabilities, and other factors of damage, Americans suffered with the Oklahoma federal building bombing that killed 161 people, and destroyed the entire office building. This office building facility consisted of a massive amount of business equipment including people, and even a day care center full of children. Understanding this was the act of a man (formerly enlisted in the U.S. Army) that theoretically could not except something, or make any better decision on a discrepancy of problems, "he then took it out on" the American people of Oklahoma. Timothy McVeigh, and Terry Nicolas caused, and committed this fatal harm, and level of financial damage to a vast amount of people's lives, and therefore the state, and federal government took up a large percentage of cost, and liability. Timothy McVeigh was the angered master mind to set off the bomb causing the massive explosion upon which he has been executed for this U.S. domestic crime of terror.

Considering the duty, and helpful concept of overall government, this Oklahoma disaster of liability within domestic terror also consisted of all the logical, and factual problems of concern within the future in America. Mostly this consisted of business, social, and government conditional matters to support these terrified victims of Oklahoma. This $12 million dollar U.S. government facility in

Oklahoma, and the millions of dollars of equipment in the facility was a complicated loss that also injured some people critically for life. Following this government disaster, the facility was then demolished. Also other chronological facts around the times of 1995, the United States citizens, and the federal government suffered the loss of 2 members of the United States Congress, and the U.S. Commerce Secretary Ron Brown in fatal airplane crashes. This was a liability problem that seemed to have issues of severe negligence within how these discretionary accidents of insecurity occurred. This was a large blow, and factor of harmful looking negligence that more than likely could have been prevented.

The Oklahoma Alfred P Murrah federal building disaster, and the fatal airplane crash of U.S. Commerce Security Ron Brown, and certain staff members was a severe loss with conditions of liability within the United States federal government. This tragedy, was slightly similar to the sad losses of President John Kennedy, and the Reverend Martin Luther King considering a valid amount of things had to be reconsolidated. These very slow reconsolidation changes occurred by making plans with vital decisions of these issues that consisted of important factors of liability, and overall security. Even as the American society was approaching the millennium year of 2000 that consisted of major oil spill clean up's, flood damages, corporate, and government fraud legal matters, and the bad of all foreign relations that occurred with the September 11, 2001 terrorist hi-jacking attacks, these where overall problems of liability, and U.S. National Security concerns. Upon the fact of killing hundreds (100s) of people on 4 separate airplanes, and the destruction of both New York World Trade Center buildings with thousands of people killed inside, and outside of this facility, nothing was left standing. This also includes issues of unsecured liability, and the evaluated damage with certain severe social effects which became tremendous. This was factual harm of a terrorist attack that had our American people, and tax paying society observant with concern. In addition a severe amount of damage, and fatalities was caused at the United States Department of Defense (the Pentagon) facility near Washington D.C. causing complications of harm, and financial liabilities.

During the year of 2005 a British Petroleum Co. (c/o Amoco) facility suffered a massive explosion killing 14 people, injuring a hundred other people, and costing billions of dollars in damage. This oil refinery was not factored on a similar level as the 9-11 "Report of Terror" attacks, but this was truly an American domestic issue of disaster. The concept and consideration of this terror report issue included mostly international issues of hate against America, and some U.S. domestic matters of complicated liabilities. Therefore within all of these conflicts that the American system of government had to consolidate within a large scale condition of disaster, and a resourceful government commitment, enforcement issues of liability become vitally relevant. These have become some of the most disastrous years for certain oil company's upon which some have restructured, and more so airline businesses (c/o United Airlines Corporation) which have suffered over the last decade and a half up to 2010. Observing, and somewhat understanding this conflict, help was applied where certain problems were evident, and therefore these needed corrections "came" slightly too late.

These clearly destructive attacks (c/o some negligence) against government, corporations, and the people over the years of 1990 to 2005 have been a serious factor of problems. Within our American society of business, and social conditions of respectful agreements, and disagreements we as American's have lost observation of society within protecting our short term, and long term Anti-Trust disciplines of liability. Even from the observation that the state, and federal courts of the United States, America has fallen behind in prosecuting case's that may have prevented certain crimes, and severe "fatal, and financial negligence". This formal conflict of issues included damage to the people, and the American society that become occasionally disastrous. This is sustained by the people, and business owners whom must find ways to hold financial business operating stability. Lately during the end of the first 2000 decade these financial matters was partly the cause of a recession throughout these factual times of procrastinated economic, and financial market values. Considering most businesses with an effort to expand these resources within certain markets, have been a real harmful subject of liability to certain business procedures. Also within the format of hearing case's that consist of the technological difference that clearly violate the U.S. Constitutional Rights of American citizens, these where issues of technology that theoretically had been used wrongfully.

A liability factor of all technology, and science including scientific principals in the United States is to be used in a lawful way that is consistent with the United States Constitution. Considering these important factors this means individuals, and business owners where destroyed as victims by legal statements of insecure and procrastinated "statues of limitations". Then with no regulated government "technological, scientific, and theological" discipline's that where not being regulated or enforced certain social problems would get worse. The real problem occurred when certain lawyers, and government prosecutors would say we don't enforce some conditional laws for citizens, or small business owners. This became the complacent statement of manipulation within complex contingent liabilities, especially as it applies to what these prosecutors could have done to prevent the 9-11 terrorist attacks. This is something we must endure with close economic observation, and then live with to understand correcting these individual business, market, and social problems of concern lawfully, and to have local productivity in most regions.

Before the massive multi-billion dollar issue of damages that occurred after the 2005 Hurricane Katrina in Mississippi, and Louisiana a vast amount of courts were rewarding settlements on hot spelt coffee at McDonald's restaurants. Also a vast amount of large compensation rewards for woman working in certain manufacturing facilities "if some were really working", where rewarded with conflicting financial court settlements. Although a few woman throughout the United States in the 1990s, and 2000s have been treated worse than woman in the 1970s, and 1980s. These were issues which now some conflicts have gotten as bad as the treatment of woman in certain parts of the Middle East with public beatings. Observing this concern the consideration that men and woman still must maintain a more productive, and respectful working relationship is vital. Manipulation of employment when favoring woman over some men on certain jobs has factored a long-term problem if employment duties where not maintained productively, and this sometimes means that anything goes including foreign conflicts of interest. This occasionally is rewarding discriminatory fraud that hurts the U.S. economy that we have strongly observed.

As we work to believe within the difference of fraudulent legal issues we observe that medical malpractice, and workplace liability issues have not been a legal court concern when some doctors seem to need to be corrected for their mistakes. Without lawfully, and ethically correcting these problems by professionals, and certain businesses, the American society moves more so backwards. This is the factual consideration of rightful compensation with productive concerns for the damages suffered by the patient-victim, and citizens affected by social conflicts that hopefully don't lead to violence. This includes even how people are affected by certain volatile weather that could have had less damage or fatalities that the people physically endure with injuries, and damages. These are victimized and financial expense concerns that push victims and the American economy into a conflicting bad direction. Then this becomes a consideration of long-term management concerns that cause a negative effect on sometimes small businesses. Therefore it is a problem when various professions, and occupations within people don't put forth their best effort within workable commitments.

These factual liability problems within people also include some cases of instigated "Insurance Fraud" before September 11, 2001, and the massive hurricane, and flooding damage of the 2005 Hurricane Katrina. Although there are some good hard working people in most of America's judicial circuit court jurisdictions, only certain issues within massive evidence of destructive damages have severely been taken as judicial notice. Most insurance companies, and other businesses with questionable support from the state and federal governed courts could not afford or make effort (c/o complacency) against a consistent fault too compensate a factor of multiple counts or acts of fraud. This compounded issue of crime without governed enforcement was most times against the good of American law practice professionals, and client's which most lawyers try to serve. This means some courts where eliminating the possible good people suffering from criminal infractions of critical legal conflicts applicable to their business, and or personal lives. These issues become something that can possibly be bad considering the future array of other calculated problems. Basically this consisted of convicting some people of things that were not even passed as law.

Certain law and other professional issues such as within the vast amount of law suits filed by the victims of the (2005) New Orleans, Louisiana "Hurricane and Floods", and even the Texas City Oil refinery explosion had preventative facts concerning various conflicts, and issues that lingered. Negligence, unprofessional conduct, and some issues of intent to instigate or commit a crime where not to be ignored. Contrary to these facts, the productive people whom were victimized from the flood disaster became part of a uncommitted, and or unproductive chain of industry, and governed engineering issues of command! A vast amount of other people restructured their livelihoods, and most everything else in New Orleans. Another factor is that the people that could have help prevent various fatal disasters seem to be the hard working American's that various businesses did not want to employ. This means that they would have been able to help prevent this problem considering most solutions where far away from being considered if all precautions where part of professional, and occupational commitments.

The consideration of people victimized concerning various occupational, and professional issues have now only slightly been pursued within certain courts for legal action. These are factors upon which even humiliation within conflicting pain, and suffering in various ways was ignored by government, and some law professionals. This problem went to the extent of various people with investments, certain U.S. Securities and Exchange Commission staff officials under Chairman Chris Cox (c/o a Donald Powers) whom would tell people with complaints that the U.S. Constitution does not apply to investment bankers, and a few others. Basically this statement, and a few others including their though process was "wrong", near deadly, and destructive. These officials making this statement to certain people was truly part of the worse decision makers in government, or they were being paid to do nothing or not enough as government allowed financial criminals to pursue bad conflicts. This seems to be partly the complacent level of criticism which years later destroyed people's financial security. These legal matters then were pursued against the different forms of government, and businesses that caused a condition of negligence with fatalities, suffering, and other problems like financial damage. The people, government, and various insurance companies, consist of these liability issues for most steel manufacturing companies. The factor of insurance liability exist for various government structures, and even the BP Company of America in terms of the oil industry whom has only slightly suffered (c/o other industries) with these contingent liability factors.

British Petroleum (PLC) Company of America has continuously suffered, and on some occasions lacked work place safety, and liability problems between 2005 thru 2009. During 2005 which was the 2nd year for Tony Hayward as Chief Executive, these challenges for the BP Company which had increased in corporate size got slightly worse. During October of 2009 British Petroleum PLC was taken to court by the U.S. Occupational Safety and Health Administration (OSHA), and then the federal court fined BP (PLC) Company $87 million dollars. Other fines due to work place liabilities within safety for the BP Company of America where $21 million dollars, $57 million dollars, and $50 million dollars including other liability expense factor's in cost. This $87 million dollar fine (contrary to other firms) was considered by OSHA, and the courts due to various safety hazards that caused the 2005 fatal explosion at the Texas City, Texas oil refinery plant.

On April 20, 2010 the BP Company had it's second (2nd) bad accident in 5 years which consisted of their Deepwater Horizon oil rig 50 miles of the coast of Louisiana. This accident caused the death of 11 oil rig workers with others injured, and a busted pipe at the bottom of the ocean pouring millions of gallons of oil into the sea, onto the land, and on various beach areas. This also put a hold on a $2.1 trillion dollar fishing industry. Considering these factual problem's in Louisiana, and the Texas oil refinery plant that was formerly an Amoco Oil Corporation facility it consisted of certain values that have been lost in the American society. Concerning this former Amoco Oil Corporation facility in Texas before the "late 1998" buyout transaction by British Petroleum Company, these issues of devastation have become part of complacent issues that lacked American industry standards. This complacent American industry problem is not just in the oil industry, but also in other heavy manufacturing, and other chemical refinery process plants, and facilities. Therefore this is a similar issue, and problem that must be considered for corrections throughout various parts of mass production industries in America.

Understanding a massive level of damage against the people, and assets of America is the liability conflict of comparison within the Judiciary, and even the Congress of the United States with certain corrections that become vital. This is appropriate upon serving the duty of ethics, and conduct within achieving prosperity that is applicable to the Constitution of the United States. Then most all resources of the individual state governments as it applies to all types of businesses, and corporations can maintain social, and lawful values. Within our individual state governments it has been vitally important that the government's judicial prosecutors not consider or allow this to become a consistent level of instigated incompetence. This includes the potential negligence and civil crimes of damages that a person, or business person provides to the court as an advised problem, or complaint. Some judicial prosecutors have become too complacent with excuses to instigate in-competency. This is a problem that implements harm by instigating incompetence over productive or knowledgeable people, and therefore the logic of good judicial evaluations, and rulings are left unproductive.

Observing complacent issues of laziness also consist of judicial jokes, and this leaves certain people, and businesses with problems. These problems can sometimes turn into criminal court matters especially with senior citizens, and young people that become confused. Most levels of factual confusion causes a lack of disciplined resources, or no financial support considering other important decisions. The fact of this matter in these business, or social issues of conflict includes even the American's that commit defamation of character against productive or younger American people. Then, the support of foreign businesses, are occasionally creating an international problem against American individuals, government, and businesses.

The small, or large American businesses including some individuals that sometimes can be victimized by "international business" has even included factors of "international terrorism" which becomes an American domestic issue of vital concern. One vital factor is that small, and large American businesses already must respect each other, and then occasionally compete against others lawfully. If these competitive issues go right, it is sometimes healthy, and productive for the American economy. Then the American business society is compounded with additional competition from the good, and even sometimes bad international businesses that have insight of doing business in America. This has become the factor of liability, and market capitalism that American businesses must achieve including the support of citizens, and all government. It is important from time, to time for American business owners to understand how this applies to the U.S. Anti-Trust laws that include the individual states. Keeping the United States economy strong, and the U.S. Federal Constitutional laws within factual order, the rest is up to the governed capacity of the courts, and the judiciary's duty of taking lawful, and or immediate factual enforceable attention. This is even more so vitally important upon the consideration's that Americans should have an understanding, and compensate awareness of the laws of the United States better then some, or most foreign business people. Therefore our American resource of priorities will have been applied appropriate as we best understand the liability of the U.S. Constitution.

The United States Anti-Trust Laws that include the Sherman Anti-Trust Act. (1890), the Clayton Anti-Trust Act. (1914), and the Federal Trade Commission Act are reluctantly contingent, and relevant to business liabilities. Other Anti-Trust law issues are the applicable duties provided within the United States Bill of Rights. This occasionally becomes factually important to have some citizens, and businesses that apply understanding, and be appropriated with these valued rights within the legal support of most professional disciplines. It also becomes vital to understand that the United States Constitutional laws are important to be obeyed, enforced, and complied with each, and considerably everyday as best as possible. This becomes a vital part of the workable formation of our American social, and business resources of discipline.

The American society of government also has other state, and federal U.S. Anti-Trust laws that are important to observe, and recognize especially when a small business is expanding with logical conditions of productive business activity. This means that some conditions of competition can increase, but also issues of negligence in financial, fatal, and or conflicting crime can destroy certain factors of business progress including what especially exist in small businesses. The concept of U.S. Anti-Trust law issues also apply severely to the different, and many licensed professional's in society, and sometimes the people, and government concerns that these issues may consist of within lawfully competitive business. It becomes important to remember that athletic competition, and events are closely regulated by the officials at the game, and this is slightly different from business. Contrary to the different atmosphere of business competition, and business competitors with conflicts this occasionally spills over into the general public with involvement, and some people victimized. Some victims are between the considered mist of employment between two or more employees, and business competitors which sometimes cannot be pursued properly with regulation. This is a problem that the state & federal system of government must enforce; similar to U.S. Anti-Trust laws, and other legal, and government disciplines that protect the people.

The format, and concern of business competition is within the need of the state, and federal government to provide legislative amendments that appropriate the advanced business issues of today. This includes a format within these issues with the lowest concept of harmful negligence. Vitally another resource includes the observation of fair, and unfair business practices that are to be prevented by the United States Federal Trade Commission, and other government officials within how these conflicts occur today. These considerations of the changing times during certain years within the first decade of 2000 with certain existing markets, and various business conditions has included formal issues of technological oversights that require state and federal legislative concerns. Therefore the format of business liabilities within certain market business competitive differences are most times respected within the changing concept of good, and bad resources of markets, and technology. Between all business products, and services for consumers, this is a liability of importance with appropriate opinions.

How businesses in certain markets has or can violate the law against each other is occasionally complicated, but this is an important factor of bad manipulation and or conditions of liability that government has a duty to eliminate if it is out of control. This relevant issue is sometimes required within certain state, and federal laws of information disclosers, and becomes consistent in a high rate of time observed by business owners, and or employees to have within responsible acknowledgement. These are the laws to protect the integrity, and liability within the American markets of lawful responsibilities upon why the Sherman Anti-Trust Act was passed, and established by the United States Congress. This Sherman Anti-Trust Act was established to prevent monopolies illegally with restraint of trade, which more so prohibits acts or contracts tending to create certain monopoly's, and initiated an era of trust-busting. Understanding this the people, and all businesses must maintain a logical, or lawful price, and a valued system of doing business fairly within sales of products, or service. Occasionally this also includes the social values of conduct between all people respectfully. This provides governed responsibility of enforcing the Sherman Anti-

Trust Act that sometimes requires duties by the United States Federal Trade Commission, and the judiciary. Observing this, the American consumer has lawful rights as well as the responsibilities of payment obligations for product good's, and services.

This liability format between the people as consumers, and different business's within products, services, and even how advertisements are provided is within the factor that all businesses, and people that must respect these lawful disciplines, and rights of each other is of vital importance. Considering these issue's, and laws that apply to most all "State, and U.S. Federal Constitutional" disciplines of professions like accounting, law, engineering, and internal medicine becomes applicable to small businesses that occasionally expand into certain large firms. Then these firms with good professional standards are workable disciplines that have obligated differences. These business expanding issues consist of taxable hard work that will withstand these issues that consist of managed market capitalism.

Market capitalism, and the American business factors of markets (c/o SEC legal discloser, and rate capacities) within small businesses maintaining liabilities, and market strength can become what is factored as a valued public, private, corporation or a firm. During 2010, and the American economic crisis very few businesses are expanding into larger markets with certain prosperous business. As certain people, or a business person in a small business establishment pursuing a business expansion with people, and liabilities of a disciplined market level of liquidity this is part of their liquidity resource to increase values. This occasionally becomes important to outline various issues of U.S. Anti-Trust laws for liability, and obvious conditions of competitive expansion. Also to recognize the different levels of customer service apart from government disciplines within a variation of other diversified state, and federal defined subjects of business American capitalism has relevance of important details.

Actually it is the format of well operated business by people that should or do prosper from their honest hard work, and commitment to others lawfully, and with logic!

A certain amount of American people, and individual business owners that move, or direct a small business going into larger markets of liability, and liquidity has defined values. These business values with capital gains, "and growth", are part of businesses with three important terms, and definitions apart from the sole proprietor of a business, and they are "Corporation", "Incorporation", and what is a defined discipline within "Articles of Incorporation". The definition of "Corporation" is a legal entity, chartered by a U.S. (American) state government, and or recognized by the U.S. federal government. It is also separate, and distinct from the persons who own it; giving rise to a jurist's remark that it has neither a "soul to condemn" nor a "body to kick". Nonetheless, it is regarded by the courts (c/o different business people) as an artificial person; it may own property, incur debts, sue, or be sued. The term "Corporate" has three chief distinguishing features: one is its limited liability within owners that can only lose what they financially invest. Two, the corporation has easy transfer of ownership rights through the sale of shares of stock. The third is that, the corporation has an ongoing business continuity of existence. Within this format of definitions there are other social, product, and service factors helping explain the corporation's ability to profit from the growth of business.

The other defined business establishment is the status of "Incorporation" and the concept of Articles of Incorporation. A factual definition of "Incorporation" is the process upon filing by which a company receives a state government charter allowing it to operate as a corporation. The fact of incorporation must be acknowledged in the company's legal name, using the word incorporated, the abbreviation (Inc.) or other acceptable variations. A defined concept, and factual definition of Articles of Incorporation" is an outlined document filed with a U.S. (American) state government by the founders of the corporation. After approving the articles, the state government issues a Certificate of Incorporation; the two divided and the concentration of documents together become the charter that gives the corporation it's legal existence. The charter embodies such information as the corporation's name, purpose, amount of authorized shares, and the number, and diversity of directors, and board members. The corporation's powers are thus derived from the "laws of the state" (c/o government), and from the provisions of the charter. Rules governing its internal management set forth in the corporations "By-Laws" which become important and applicable to amendments are drawn up by the founders. Therefore these become very important subjects, and issues of filing duties within the format of a business being a good, and productive corporate, and business citizen. This is the format within the observation, and disciplines of state government, and some U.S. federal regulatory concerns that occasionally have responsibilities that include lawful commerce.

The individual state governments, and the United States federal government most times recognize these levels of small, and large business conditions that are established as a corporation, or a business format of incorporation including some sole proprietors. Upon business issues including most documented Articles of Incorporation these are the duties that the management, and chief executives of these businesses pursue best, considering what makes the business operate productively inside, and out. All levels of business inputs are measured, and this produces the good, and bad of business outputs that includes the state, and federal tax base that provides us all a money circulation within government services. Understanding this the long range of business products, and services with the many different American businesses that are governed, and factored with liability, this becomes vitally important within the long term conditions of business.

The consideration of long term business in certain American markets is sometimes best described within the professional term of a "Holding Company's rights, and disciplines" of active business. A holding company is observed, and defined in a few various ways. The "Holding Company" has some consistent values similar to a corporation that owns enough voting stock in another corporation to influence its policies, and management. A holding company need not own a majority of the stock shares (c/o bonds) of its subsidiaries, or be engaged in similar activities. However, to gain the benefits of tax consolidation, which includes tax-free dividends to the parent company, and the ability to share operating losses, the holding company must own 80% or more of the subsidiaries voting stock. Within the observed good, and bad of business activity, the advantage of a holding company over a "Merger" as an approach to expansion are the ability to control sizeable operations with fractional ownership. In addition the commensurately of small investments; "meaning some people are part of working investors is an important subject upon knowledgeable people within controlling the ownership of the company. This is somewhat theoretically "the astute" ability to take risk through subsidiaries with liability limited to the subsidiary corporation; then the people, employees, and business consist of liable factors. Considering this, a format, and the ability to expand through unobtrusive purchases of stock is valued in contrast to having to obtain the approval of another company's shareholders.

Other good, and bad business activities within the disadvantages of a holding company are a partial multiple taxation when less than 80% of a subsidiary is owned. Upon this format plus other special state and local taxes; the risk of forced "Divestiture" (it is easier to force dissolution of a holding company then to separate a merger operation c/o laws); and the risk of negative leverage effects in excessive pyramiding, or liquidity. This was the effect of various (c/o American) corporate buyouts within banking which included Wells

Fargo buying Wachovia Bank, and especially British Petroleum Companies buyout of Amoco Oil Corporation upon which a negative leverage effect consisted of excessive liquidity problems. Certain markets within businesses in the United States consist of certain types of holding companies that are defined in most of these special ways. Then these business concerns are subject to particular legislation: the U.S. Public Utility Company Holding (Act.), U.S. Bank Holding Company (Act), U.S. Railroad Holding Company (Act), and the U.S. Air Transport Holding Company (Act).

Understanding the issues of format and responsibility within our American society of business, and liabilities is the outline of maintaining markets of discipline with liabilities. These become issues of capitalism at rates that are productive for most all people that are living with good, and sometimes bad health, but prepared to work. The saddest fact within liability is that America has lost a vast amount of people, and places of employment to non-liable negligence, and what is factored of "criminal negligence, and or fatal negligence". This is a factual problem in numerous corporate manufacturing facilities that include accumulated financial damages that factor a severe cost to business. Therefore whether the business is a corporation, an incorporated entity, or a holding company that has a loss of people that consisted of a flow of damages to equipment, and the facilities, our American society of business is approaching (c/o 2009 and 2010) serious economic trouble. This also includes insurance companies, and the massive effect on the economy, and most government budgets considering all different conflicts that have to be corrected. As American citizens, and the consolidation of all professions, and occupations it becomes important to remember during the 1929 Great Depression, business and individuals suffered from something that was slightly though to be impossible, or strange. Now during the year of 2008, and just because the Great Depression of 1929 that is within the concept of 78 years ago, the economy, and format of businesses today can suffer the same effect if not possibly worse. What is financially and socially considered as the worse may not happen due to some newly set up laws to control certain volatile market activity. Then contrary to all markets within all logical, and possible factors it is vital to not ignore, or sign off what could be a serious economic repercussion, and how to survive it.

Liability In Banking And Investment Banking
(7)

CHAPTER SEVEN
(7)

The United States Library of Congress

Liability In Banking And Investment Banking
(7)

The business concept, and discipline within markets, public, and private businesses including various types of organizations, and individuals of all ages throughout America severely depend on the American society of banking, and the perceptional use of investment banking. Within the largest to the smallest banking establishments observing the local, state, and federal levels of banks, their conditions of liability within money transactions, and services has always become a vital American business necessity. The concept of this also includes the important factors of laws, and the circumference of business, and personal banking activities that are used at massive rates by the American general public.

The consolidation of banking establishments has changed in many ways over the last 100 years, and that includes the different services, and ways that banks and their depositors are secured, and protected. Most, but not all banking establishments in the United States of America are lawfully registered with the United States Federal Reserve Bank system (headquartered in Washington D.C.), which is an important local or commerce bank "supervisor of regulation, and constituency". Contrary to the fact, and duties of the U.S. Federal Reserve Bank upon whom the last few Chairman's where Paul Volker, and Alan Greenspan (over 25 years) is the most lawfully established, and governed bank supervisor system in America. These chairman's of the United States Federal Reserve bank are appointed by the President of United States with conformation hearing's from the U.S. Congress that has presently appointed Ben Bernanke during the year of *2006. Considering different banks, and their discretion of banking services that is observant at most all banks, the Federal Deposit Insurance Corporation (FDIC) was established to ensure a level of "insured deposited funds" for American bank customers. This concept with the FDIC, the United States Federal Reserve Bank, and some others are vital parts of the liability issues of liquidity values within the American banking industry.

Banking is the business of receiving, protecting, and the lending of money in a lawful, professional and ethical way including the business capacity disciplines that exist in America, and in various different parts of the world. Observing commerce banking in America the concept of international banking is supervised thru the World Bank which is headquartered in Washington D.C., and it also holds evaluated recommendations from the United Nations in New York, and the United States government. This bank regulates, and supervises international lending and more so currency rates that applies to the banking matters of the United Nations worldwide. This is considered helpful by all ages of young, and old people in developing countries. Additional function's coordinated by the World Bank is the various activities for the International Monetary Fund (IMF), the International Finance Corporation, and a few other detailed entities like the Children Defense Fund, and International Disaster Relief funds.

Most bank (Holding Company) establishments maintain liability banking procedures that are prescribed in law by the Bank Holding Company Act, and a vast amount of other banks that are regulated by the National Bank Act, and the Federal Reserve Act. After the economic Depression of 1929 the Banking Act of 1933 was fractionally productive with government conditions of the establishment for the Federal Deposit Insurance Corporation (FDIC) to govern economic, and financial banking matters. This creation of the FDIC was established to help banks, and the bank depositors maintain different market, and insured money management issues. During the 1990s up until now during the years of 2006, and 2007 a vast amount of the commerce banking establishments, investment banks, and the concept of mortgage lending banks have suffered. These difficult times going into 2009 existed from credit delinquency accounts, and certain factors of banking within mortgage loan payments which have "lately" left the American economy with a problem it must recover from. The year 2007 has accumulated some of the worse loan collection years in decades. Contrary to this fact as we may observe, or understand the meaning of the "bank holding company" laws they were established for the maintaining of stable bank ownership, and most bank business operating conditions that could consist of losses within equity, and liquidity. Various issues have been supported by the United States government which consisted of a level of protection that exist at the FDIC for the depositor's, but in some conditions the overall economy has been part of this tremendous greed, conflict, and other problems like discretionary corporate mergers.

A bank holding company usually has a format of owning, or maintaining the control of two, or more banks, or other bank holding companies. As defined in the Bank Holding Company Act of 1956, such companies must register with the Board of Governors of the U.S. Federal Reserve Bank System, and hence are called registered bank holding companies. Amendments to the 1956 Act set standards for acquisitions (1966), and ended the exemption enjoyed by one-bank holding companies (1970), thus registering bank holding companies to consist of the activities related to the banking industry. Considering the year of 2008 a factual concept of these federal mandated laws, and acts have been part of a reorganized factor from disastrous spending, and fraud within the American society. The logic of this problem got worse observing the factual good, and bad of foreign issues, including domestic lending practices.

Understanding the markets of different types of special lending bank concerns within establishments has been factually important to their recent concept of arbitration for the best concern to maintain long-term economic discipline. These factors of arbitration within certain new banking procedures have good, and bad issues considering if a bank can maintain long-term progress. In this day in time this seems conflicting whether the bank last longer than 25 years, 5 years, or even a year in our American society of bank businesses. Observing this, most banks become a long-term discipline that must be managed properly. This banking format of today considerably is observed by reason that this industry still has bank business law's, and liabilities with special features at individual banks. Theoretically some of these bank facilities (contrary to an establishment) may have been considered "FLY BY NIGHT Banking JOINTS". This is "theoretically" because of the high loan interest rates, and a lack of business including employment stability! Inadvertently in a more concerned factor of resources this arbitration liability consist of the factual observation of even how the concept of college student loans, and certain business lending has been increased with some government programs. These programs and a variety of other loans make a format of tax dollar circulation with repayment liability's valuable which appropriates the concept of leveraged commitments that must be considered properly on most all occasions. These special lending issues considering the need for college studies are different from grants that consist of a severe consideration of loan options to the outline of stable payments. This appropriates the good, and more so occasionally uncertain or closely manipulative concept of unlawfully bad loan rates, and agreements that are vital to individual decision making.

Understanding, and observing the complexity of the liability within American banking issues, the variety within American banking conflicts, and the variety of American citizens as customers has diversified issues, and values they must apply discipline for with the best results. This especially includes when some college students of an older age own a home, and other assets that must be paid for within time, and with agreed commitments considering there is a logical format to follow. Some lenders have closed their businesses, and sold accounts to other lenders, or collection agents, and then raised the rates for the consuming people that borrowed. This is occasionally where the good of stable banking establishments including government programs consist of certain levels of good, and bad disciplines of arbitration, and closely unregulated business decision making.

Observing certain factual business duties, the provision of bank lending procedures must be lawfully factored within liability to the depositor, and customers with respect to the bankers. In certain documents that I entitled as the Endless Loop Crisis, I explained certain investment bank legal concerns with certain bills that must be paid along with earnings of income in productive professions such as engineering, computer programming, accounting, and others. This legal issue is also applicable to the understanding of one's personal expenses, and certain small productive business matters to make future long-term commitments productive. Observing certain facts of investment banking in America a large capacity of margin account investments fell behind for a large group of investors during the late 1990s. This occasionally also means financial, and economic trouble for some banking establishments as well more so investment brokers. Therefore American citizens of all kinds from college students to older professionals, and certain investors including some business owners suffered from these personal and business investment activities. These observed issues of format become part of good, and bad issues of American markets, and the liquidity that exist in the banking industry that has closely taped a (2008) financial, and economic recession.

The rules, regulations, and factors of liability within commerce bank establishments, and more so investment bank concerns for these business conditions of banking is slightly different, but both have their similarities. Within observing this American market some of these similarities are consistent to savings, checking, and money market accounts upon managing combined banking matters. Concerning the rule's, and regulation of investment bank's including investments that are strictly observed, and governed with the Securities and Exchange Commission (SEC) of the United States government, extensive review of all activities is a vital duty. Throughout the years there has been numerous people prosecuted within the concept of the SEC financial markets of logical business, and some issues of greed. Observing the United States Securities and Exchange Commission (SEC) sense 1990 the revolving door of the SEC Chairman position has consisted of Richard Breeden, Arther Levitt, Harvey Pitt, William Donaldson, Chris Cox, and presently Mary Schapiro which has been a turnover rate higher than most federal chairmanship officials.

Understanding this high turn-over rate of the SEC position of chairman it looks like an "endless loop crisis", and a high volume of financial transactions that consisted of argumentative concerns. Observing stability with business or employment income to invest money in brokerage accounts along with a saving or checking account continuation process of social, and financial values, some conflicts consist of certain American values that have been threatened. These are financial resources that the SEC, and the Federal Reserve Bank should be lawfully disciplined with concerning an attorney, and with strong concerns of various government constituents which applies to the lawful managing, and investing of money. These government constituents consist of the SEC, the Federal Reserve Bank, and others such as Attorney Generals have duties to observe the important concerns, and details of these matters to seek resolution.

This is also similar to bank regulating issues due to the fact that the U.S. Federal Reserve Bank board members and chairman consist of an office managed by these people within appointed positions to serve the citizens of America. Also they are responsible to be committed to the bipartisanship for all of the American people, and their commitments to banks, and regulatory issues. Considering the Federal Reserve Chairman Position, and board members upon their federal guideline duties their appointments consist of 14 year terms. These terms have a timing of sustainable factors which help understand the good, and bad of any up's, and down's the American economy may endure.

Observing economic justice considering all kinds of high, and low levels of financial crimes that needed to be prosecuted, these factors of greed must be corrected by the people, and government even more so to manage various financial equation's. This type of unlawful activity most times hurts a vast amount of businesses that work along the line of fair, and lawful activities of business, banking, investment banking, planning, and achieving personal, and business goals. Sometimes financial crimes, and issues of financial negligence occur, and the liability of most investment bank conditions within these subjects are not insured, but upon complained factors, and probable cause in the courts. Considering these issues with other American factors of business, and individual social value's these government observed resources become important duties. Also considering negligence, and or crime against the rules, regulation, and corporate "By-Laws" in the capacity of corporate operating standards, and large brokerage firms it is occasional that large rewards are compensated for certain damages. Large engineering, law, and accounting firms consist of similar lawful rules, and disciplined factors which also can be recognized in their professional codes of conduct, and values within business ethics. Therefore the liability seems to be a 50-50 on some investment legal issues if victims will financially survive any, and all conditions of certain financial crimes.

Most corporate, and investment bank constituency conflicts, concerns, and issues are within the relevance of markets, businesses, and the liability within some local banking. Considering some of the largest banks in the world exist in the United States, the formal concept of banking as a business is a consolidation for all citizens, businesses, organizations, others, and various people of different ages, and estate conditions. This means all ages of people including those with different resources of banking know where their money is, and the logical procedures to receive portions of it when the money is needed upon management, and liability. What has made some banks popular, and productive is that their concept of doing business with rules of high standards of liability "that can relieve worries" has included the earnings of interest on money saved. Understanding the interest rates of today, the people (c/o depositors) with money saved, and these factors of prosperity within liquidity can create stronger asset liquidity if all things go right with most social, and business concerns.

The format within markets of investment banks, and other types of banks in America are similar, but the valued difference within rates of interest, and the review of regulated laws to provide different types of money management instruments, and or investments has variations. This is the format of bank business decisions within the liability discipline of banks to offer businesses, individuals, and or investors the consideration of their most logical best services. Certain examples are the different services between banks such as Bank of America, Citibank (a subsidiary of Citigroup), or the consolidation of Fidelity Investments, Merrill Lynch, Goldman Sachs, and others which includes how the Glass-Steagall Act of 1933 was to help govern, and provide a legal separation of the banking industry that consist of regulative issues of importance. This legal discipline of bank business market resources within the Glass-Steagall Act clearly appropriated legal security for the depositors of commercial banking. Considering this fact the money management laws within service of the local, or federal bank issued facts within goals, and procedures are diversified, and different subjectively. Therefore this is a procedure from the investment bank to insure that the American values within client / customer issues are maintained within their format of logical sacrifice's, and banking goals.

The Glass-Steagall Act is defined as legislation passed by the Congress of the United States authorizing deposit insurance, and prohibiting commercial banks from owning brokerage firms. Under the Glass-Steagall Act, these banks are not to engaged in investment banking activities, such as the duties of underwriting corporate securities, or municipal revenue bonds. The law was designed to insulate bank depositors from the risk involved when a bank dealt in securities, and to prevent a collapse like the one that occurred during the 1920s in the Great Depression. In the mid-1980s certain banks pursued the challenge's of the Glass-Steagall Act by offering money market funds, discount brokerage services, commercial paper, and other investment opportunities. This good, and more so bad fact of challenges is still active with other banking, and business complex issues that must be considered by the Congress, and or legislative amendments.

Some banks have reorganized this concerned discrepancy of bank business regulated procedures, and activities within the lawful way this is helpful to personal, and business banking. Besides checking, saving, and loan accounts now some regular, or local banks only offer the highest grade of investments consisting of "Bonds, and Certificates of Deposits". Considering these banking establishments that offer Certificates of Deposits, U.S. Treasury Bonds, and even U.S. Savings Bonds, this has created banking with safe, and secure conditions. A difference of factor's exist within all conditions of a challenge concerning some bank establishment's that have continued usually possessing (2) two similar bank names. This is done to offer investment or financial banking service's which these issues require lawfully aggressive concerns, but with conduct, and ethical decisions. Observing this, the regular bank service duties that appropriate the valid risk described in the Glass-Steagall Act, certain matters are due with corrections.

The consideration of a combined regular local bank, and an investment bank has been observed to do some things that convert, and expand most banking services, but this also has suffered within various bank funded subjects of economic stability. This includes the reallocating of funds due to margin accounts that consist of good, and bad investments, and occasional market differences of expansion. A vast amount of banks today excluding the United States Federal Reserve Bank system, and a few others that do not heavily engage in investment banking activity, this appropriates stable banking for local people. The banking establishments that have decided over the last 10 to 15 years or after 1993 for the fact that the stock market had recently established circuit breakers for volatile trading days, is part of the diversified challenge. Therefore some regular local banks that are providing investment banking services have lobbied government, or consolidated business to do so with the belief that the financial markets will never crash at the rate of 1929.

The United States (American) economy over the vast amount of decades before the 1970s, and 1980s has proven, and shown the good, and bad of market activity, and the concept of bank issues of liquidity. Some examples consist of the 1982, and 1983 Continental Bank of Chicago, Illinois whom after certain quarters of bad loan collection rates defaulted, and a run on the bank occurred. This was a severe process including loan delinquencies, and this led the Continental of Bank of Chicago banking company to the suffering concept of filing bankruptcy with other issued problems. This concept of banking, and market factors of concern also consist of the economic challenges for banking officials, and others that will speculate hypothetically whether certain market conditions will never get to certain bad levels again, is consensually irrelevant. The concept of speculation, and the estimating of bank business earnings becomes a legally important tool in these public-private owned businesses, and most serious minded market issues. Collection from loans including the input, and output of interest rates is the bank professional discipline that appropriates greater value in the asset, and liquidity management within banks, and all other business concerns. These are things within business including good decisions that professional's pursue within the logical factor of understanding what the operating cost of projected expenses, sales, and earnings will be as the businesses have planned for different goals.

Considering the concept of banks such as Citibank, and the differences within what occurred to the Continental Bank of Chicago, Illinois there is a diversified condition of management values. These bank management duties, values, and levels of bank business procedures also consist of input, and output values on interest rates. A consolidated fact within banking regions, and federal districts is the comparison that Citibank (one of the largest U.S. banks) is a Northeastern American region bank, and the Harris Bank of Chicago that is a Midwestern American region bank which both cross the resource of a vast amount of industries. Upon these regional banks, and other regions of banking this is a consolidated issue for "customers, and client's" on how these banks have some Federal Reserve District bank geographical concerns. Considering what use to be the largest U.S. mid-west bank in Illinois, the Continental Bank of Chicago "that doesn't exist for banking any more" was the seventh largest American Bank. Before their failure this bank had well over a hundred billion dollars in managed assets.

Observing the U.S. Federal Banking District of Illinois including the vast amount of Harris Bank, and Continental Bank locations during the late 1970s, and early 1980s the massive steel industry suffered financially within the people, and businesses. The U.S. Federal Reserve Bank discount window activity, and the duty of regulating commerce banking in their government facility in Chicago was a close business ally within this good, and bad money circulation. Contrary to the bank managing of interest rates that the Continental Bank pursued, a vital consideration consisted of people, and depositor's closer to certain steel manufacturing facilities, and offices in northern Indiana, and Illinois. The concern that managing the rates of account interest may suffer small detailed problems is critical, but it becomes even worse when other industries, and businesses slow down, and the bank has other commitments. With this rate of slow business, other problems (with banking) occurred that caused challenges to the lay-off of employed people. They then were subjected to readjusting various financial business conflicts, and other social problems that can accumulate financial waste, and or long-term delinquent commitments.

Banking establishments of the United States are required by (state & federal) law to set aside legal reserves of (cash holding) assets. Just like any other business when less money is being generated, earned, or collected monthly by the bank, and other businesses these assets must be used as cash reserve for the concept of business operating liquidity. Also their reserved money for operating expenses, and other financial leverage matters occasionally cause lower business profits, and earnings when certain economic factors are struggling. This is a factor within the U.S. diversified industries, and businesses including markets between New York, Houston, Los Angeles, and Chicago with other massive populated cities that consist of various important business issues. Therefore all bank establishments are important, but on various occasions large cities usually accommodate a vast amount large market business concerns that bank's appropriate a relationship with, and this applies to all good, and bad issues to be lawfully governed.

Considering all businesses that make productive efforts that help the American economy, this is a vital part of the "Gross National Product" (GNP) and or "Gross Domestic Product" (GDP) rating system. These issues of GNP or GDP rates must maintain a logical capacity of sales, and the rate of products made or manufactured including services with American people working productively. These rates more so within product's of a workable American society is valued from logical organizations of business which also help the American currency rates, and this provides stability of certain bank rates. This usually applies to the overall American economy. These production rates are also applied to the banking industry similar to most other manufactured goods, and within this format it becomes diversified in the many regions of America that must evaluate certain economic, and production matters of condition.

Citibank's market discipline on the east coast of the United States seemed to endure a more valid business, and market condition of stability during the 1970s, and 1980s. This is consolidated within certain GNP and or GDP rates which is valued from their annual business profits, and earnings from bank loan collection procedures. When bank loans are paid at productive rate's this gives the bank a "lawful, and logical" incentive to keep bank rates low for various people to borrow money, and even save money with earned interest. Upon observation of different bank issues of good, and bad profits, and earnings Citibank (c/o Citigroup) has an active condition within "investment business" procedures that form time to time has maintained stability. This seems to exist because the (Bank-Broker) Citigroup is factored to be the parent company of the bank subsidiary business of Citibank. During a hearing in 2009 Goldman Sachs Co. declared themselves to be a commerce bank apart from their vast amount of financial brokers, and financial market activity of business involvement. Observing this 2 name bank constituency, the difference is within the Glass-Steagall Act, and the risk factors to the depositing customers. This is the formality that seems to consist of where an investment brokerage or "financial services" firm owns part, or the majority of the regular, local, or commercial bank of one such as Citibank.

Observing bank business liability, and the managing of liquidity in a business which includes some non-liquid assets in commercial or local banking establishments leading up to the years of 2007, and 2008 diversified problems occurred. Considering the combination of commerce banks, and more so investment banks a certain percentage of these problems occurred from junk bonds, and margin account factors that exceeded cash, and repayment capacity limitations, or requirements. This is due to the mortgage lending economic conditions, and certain margin account losses upon which bad decisions were made. Margin lending, and the crisis within mortgage backed securities, and mortgage loan problems for certain investment banks became evident, and more so within Countrywide Bank, and the many bank purchases of Wachovia Bank. This was a diversified cash reserves issue that was part of planning for liquidity advancements from invested collateralized debt obligations. Wachovia Bank purchased 2 or 3 smaller banks within the southern regions of the United States, and therefore the merger / junk bond process gave them the good, and then a more so bad concept of financial crisis within problems. This increase in bank business assets means that Wachovia Bank, and smaller banks had additional responsibility to manage, and be liable for within liquidity, and business assets applicable also to government. Also these banking issues, and the economy were effected by certain geographical economic regional concerns that where factored with complex future earning potential. Considering these factors the asset evaluation's, and concerns of depositors was a severe concentration of bank establishment matters to survive.

A small banking establishment within the First Jefferson Bank of Biloxi, Mississippi was bought out by South Trust Banking

Corporation of Alabama. Then the Alabama bank of South Trust Banking Corporation was bought out by North Carolinas Wachovia Bank in 2004, upon which this was part of a vicious uncontrolled junk bond, and merger market. This was a different financial junk bond, and merger market then what some people observed during the late 1980s which was factored within different corporate manufacturing stocks, and company's being bought out. A professional observation would include also to look close within the bank merger of "Chemical Bank, and Manufacturing Hanover Bank" which consisted of an accumulated deal of over $135 billion dollars during the early 1990s. Now during 2008 going into 2009 Wachovia Bank has been considered into a position that they must except a buyout offer from Citigroup Incorporated, or Wells Fargo Bank observing that the company's stock value has decreased in value by 91% in less than one year.

The liquidity of a bank or business is vital just as the name of the banking institution that creates the liability of lawful significance. Wachovia Bank Corporation being a company with more than 16,000 broker's, and other businesses such as investment services has vital institutional responsibilities. Upon this observation of 16,000 brokers working for a commerce bank the Glass Steagall Act comparing 1933 and 2008 have important comparison's, even as it applies to government officials that where to enforce this law, and other legal or professional disciplines. This also included their "insurance and retirement" service business concerns which if you clearly observe this format of the insurance market liability issues of today these are some of their most severe times, and factors of the 2000 decade with financial difficulties. Most, but not all insurance businesses are at levels that have critically hurt the earnings of most insurance market matters, but these business activities are suffering from an overload of damages to financially compensate individuals, and businesses. This is a fact from the 2000 half a decade record braking insurance claims that had to be paid out. Observing this consideration of insurance company's and investment banking businesses, the consideration of liabilities has also been part of various bank merger issues. In addition they change the names of banks rapidly within liability, and ownership factors that are applicable within disclosers of questionable, and some logical resource. The concept of name changes, and mergers are within a vast amount of business good, and bad procedures considering this has implemented activity for those such as within small banks like the Lebanon Bank that was more than a half century old.

In 1987 the First Tennessee National Bank Corporation with its established management from Memphis, Tennessee acquired the small bank business establishment of Lebanon Bank for $31 million dollars. Then during 2004 First Tennessee changed the name of the bank to First Horizon National Corp. (banking), and this therefore was expanding their business to operate in 40 different states selling mortgages, and home equity loans during an interesting new construction building market expansion. During the same quarterly period of Wachovia's institutional problems First Horizon National Banking Corporation consisted of stock values that went from over $45.00 dollars a share in 2007, and then during mid-2008 to selling at $9.00 to $8.00 dollars a share. They lost most of their established value from a corporate merger to venture into a questionable financial market. In a normal bank market in America banking, the banking stock price values hold quite steady occasionally for years with appropriate managed issues, and paying secured dividends. This is the observation within some of the most recent issues of concern that are occasionally, and tremendously different.

How the liquidity, and liability within markets, business, and even what some professionals consider as the financial arbitration within businesses that includes corporate, and bank business relations, it becomes appropriate to observe the banking issue that occurred at Enron Corporation. These Enron Corporation banking issues were full of complicated market gains, and then severe losses, legal problems, and then bankruptcy. Some legal clams at the Enron Corporation observed financial troubles that amounted to about $65 billion dollars in unidentified losses reviewed between 2001, and 2005. During the same time of bank business matters with the Enron Corporation while being summoned to court, a part of their liquid assets consisted of a reported $2.2 billion dollar settlement. This settlement within liquidity of assets came from "JPMorgan Chase Bank" Company that was included with a $2 billion dollar settlement that came from "Citigroup". Considering these banks had to relieve $4.2 billion dollars of some $65 billion dollars (c/o Enron) to the Board of Regents at the University of California (c/o others) these corporate business issues including banking establishment's compiled issues of complex liquidity.

The WorldCom business, and legal factor of financial issues consisted of $180 billion dollars of market capital before it liquefied or evaporated into nothing, and then into in the bankruptcy process, and the courts. Observing these types of financial losses for some investors that have had money in certain bank accounts, the United States governments help is limited, except for the enforcement of criminal fraud matters. Upon this complicated effect of some government, and business issues, the (U.S. Gov) Federal Deposit Insurance Corporation on regular or local bank accounts guarantees up to $100,000.00 dollars. Now the U.S. guaranteed insured bank limit is being considered at around $250,000.00 as a regulatory discipline for American bank depositors. Upon this factor it means that the U.S. government and the FDIC had to insure the guarantee of more deposited money due to the high rate of bank closures. This is the liability guaranteed by the U.S. Congress, and government that these funds are Backed By The Full Faith & Credit of the

United States Government. Contrary to these factors of when banks, and businesses get in trouble at certain levels of insecurity, then this is the concern of "good and bad" business decisions upon factual risk, failure, or reward.

Most of these bank conditions of laws, and responsibilities within most all banking procedures is observed as a managing duty of the comptroller. The comptroller is the bank officer who controls all financial records, and supervises the bookkeeping, auditing, and the accounting concerning the bank. Both Enron, and WorldCom Corporations were focused on domestic, and considerably some international business activities like a few other American corporations, and businesses. These business matters become relevant facts that are occasionally overlooked. This vitally includes when dealing with foreign businesses, governed relations, and the disciplines that apply to the laws observing most "Corporate America" values, some business issues can, and has suffered differently. Occasionally this includes use of the International Monetary Funds (IMF) that is part of the international aid, and other foreign related cost issues. Therefore some foreign business factors achieved more from the lack of discipline, and American banking being directed by Enron Corporation, and WorldCom Corporation more than American small investors (c/o some who loss more than investments), and businesses consisting of volatile trading, and decision making conflicts.

Considerably good, and bad business issues, and various factors need to be observed carefully. In 1934 the Export-Import Bank was founded in Washington D.C., and now within certain transformed disciplines of markets, and business the United States government maintains the lawful control of the World Bank in New York City. This means that export-import companies doing business on an international, or global capacity are understood within foreign currency rates, and other financial and banking transitions of values.

The factor of what goes on in certain (NYC) business concerns including the United Nations governed agenda's which is becoming a logical good, and occasionally more so bad factor of these international issues is a relevant indicator of concern. Good and bad foreign trade issues considering American domestic trade, and markets can be regulated with the appropriate U.S. Constitutional disciplines of importance to hold American monetary values. These are some of the important banking, business, and government issues of liability within our American society of today that also seems to include someone's discretionary concept of dangerous "Internet Banking" activity (c/o domestic and international regulatory security) concerns. Upon even how Internet Banking has improved, this and other unlawful activity is still a great risk for commerce, and investment banking business conditions.

The Insurance Industry And U.S. Disasters
(8)

CHAPTER EIGHT
(8)

The United States Library of Congress

The Insurance Industry And U.S. Disasters
(8)

The American people, and businesses understand the "Insurance industry", and various business concerns of insurance some- what well. This industry in America was hit hard by insurance payout concerns after, and slightly before the 2005 Hurricane Katrina, which including a vast amount of fatal manufacturing explosions, and various other recent disasters has caused economic, and social turmoil. Hurricane Katrina just happened to be one of the severe tipping factors that has changed some insurance companies for years to come that where already struggling. Most of these people (c/o some victims) might even understand that due to hurricanes, tornados, earthquakes, floods, terrorism, obsolete structures, and even household, and auto accidents this has lately taken the insurance industry as businesses to bad levels in America.

Although most diversified business levels of protection from the insurance industry throughout America has observed disasters, these problems consist of the complexity of the people, businesses, government, various regions of America, and the economy. This is based on the complex values of people, households, vehicles, businesses, and a variation of other important asset subjects. This makes the value of policy's, agreements, and responsible decisions by people an issue that applies greatly within future beneficial protection. These business concerns including the logical assistance of government observing manufacturing, and natural disasters "has reminded" society that various priorities apply to all diversified insurance company's. Insurance concerns such as this also consist of various sectors of American businesses, and the people whom really can't afford serious issues. No logical business, or small, or large city, or town in America is without the total observed resource of these insurance business concerns, but you do still have the uninsured of all kinds. This is a vital resource throughout the American society which provides the people with liabilities, and asset insured coverage that consist of a certain guaranteed resource of protection. Therefore then insurance companies can or will apply financial supportive coverage, and protection for assets, items, and even the relevance of the insured people, if their own agency or business survives.

The people that work for insurance companies are basically human, and therefore they have a life to earn a prosperous living with these commitments. Most insurance people are logical hard working American's, just like the people in America that they have a market to provide, and offer these insured policies of "financial protection" service's for with documented agreements. Considering this they have an understanding of a certain amount of things that apply to assets, and clients that surround insurance issues which people may observe as lawfully important. Upon this level of importance, people then endure these various insurance agreements for the most logical amount of coverage possible, and then applied payment to the best of their ability. The financial insured protection service problems people may endure are hurricane damage, earthquake damage, home or business flood damage, civil and or criminal law damages, and a vast amount of financial, or health conditional losses. These types of insurance damages have been increasingly active from 1995 to slightly worse in 2005, and with additional problems approaching 2011. Therefore with the American changing times of insurance complexity values, this is part of the format of documented policy business issues, and procedures that offers asset protection from an arrangement within the products, and more so some services that insurance businesses offer.

It becomes vital within the American insurance industry concerning what people would like to protect, and the many assets that can be insured, including assets that are lawfully considered upon which insurance can be purchased "on", and at the proper capacity. Considering the 1990s, and the years of 2000 various newly invented products, and service conditions as it applies to computers, and the internet consist of items with diversified conditions to be insured. Inadvertently this applies to computer software, and hardware upon which can be a terrifying concern within someone's personal data base information involved. Most logical and important insurance concerns starts with cars, and homes being insured which consist of agreements that are to be held with logical discipline. Health and life insurance exist for the logical reason that people can get sick, as well when the elderly die, or pass away and the level of expenses can be insured with beneficial control. Observing these factors, the American markets of insurance have factored some good, and bad days, including years within market activity. These become the variation of liability issues of the American society that is considering the preventative concern within most personal insurance matters, and certain catastrophic events of disaster that have changed a vast amount of peoples lives.

A factual observation of insurance conflicts is considered, and observed when the market within sales of houses, and cars is at a low rate. Considering this factual problem this concern within the lack of American new car sales was hit bad after the September 11, 2001 terrorist attacks. This also means people don't need, or buy as much insurance on these products, or assets if any. The individual states, and the United States government has laws that require a person to be insured or have auto insurance, or more so too be insured to operate most types of motor vehicles. Americas state, and federal laws (c/o the United States) for vehicles apply to be in operation on all conditions of roads, in the water, and in the sky.

This is part of the insured process within the American format of lawful order that requires all vehicles on the roads to have reliable insurance coverage for all people that operate these motor vehicles. The rules, regulations, and laws are tied closely to insurance, and this consolidates the liability of safety on the roads, and throughout other places that vehicles, and or people are required to have liable insurance coverage, and logical responsibilities. Therefore within the concept of the many conditions of damages to property, health, and life the discipline of insurance can compensate pay for the personal, home, or business asset losses, and or weather damages of losses that are suffered by a business or individual clients.

Considering our American society within the years of the late 1990s, and the first decade of 2000 the American people witnessed, and suffered with their American owned and managed assets being destroyed by the force of nature, and other conflicting events of concern. The forceful nature considering events such as hurricanes, mudslides, forest wildfires, a few earthquakes in certain regions, and a vast amount of storm water flooded regions has stun various American people, and assets. This has also made asset protection problems and complex issues a vital concern within government, and various markets similar to insurance, and even the logic of professional engineering. These become some of the people within business, and society whom can provide workable solutions during the 2000 decade, and future with logical decisions.

Another complex problem includes a normal capacity of tornados that have factored, and applied unlivable conditions to various parts of America. These regions within being "State and Federal Declared Disasters", which consisted of severely damaged assets of lawful property had vital personal, and insured issues of cost, and then people have loss or had to restructure. Understanding this process it clearly becomes important that certain "extensive" conditions of property value must be adjusted. The items of value (c/o some insured) would include vehicles, houses, or other non-replaceable items, or assets.

Closely understanding, and observing the insurance companies of America, one of the worse financial conditions of damage that was caused to a region, was in the Gulf States regional disaster from the (2005) Hurricane Katrina that destroyed parts of Mississippi, and a vast amount of New Orleans, Louisiana. Although the United States government is committed to helping the Gulf States, and more so the recovery of New Orleans with different services, and money; a vast amount of insurance company officials are slightly puzzled with cost, and procedures. These insurance company official's, and lawyers are looking, and debating large policy damage issues that have effected residential homes, commercial facilities, and business districts that included heavily damaged assets. This process is slightly different because more lawyers are involved considering there is more than the normal amount of annual processing clams involved with some court proceedings.

These Gulf States regional concerns, and business issues between different insurance companies, and the vast amount of good, and bad opinions with conflicting subjects will require massive work. Within the general public, and the (state & federal) government this problem will require the determination of people, and businesses including government to closely work together with these loads of tremendous damage. The tremendous factors of damage also consist of workable cost, more asset cost, and some overtime non-factored bonuses within cost. Hopefully everything within these sacrifices will be done right, and therefore the prevention within infrastructures will be improved! It also becomes important to remember that within the Gulf States of America including Texas, Mississippi, Florida, and Louisiana (c/o New Orleans), various business markets have suffered some of these severe cost factors, and damage's.

Besides the large markets of fish, shrimp, and lobsters in these markets, there was a considerable amount of off-shore oil drilling rigs that were damaged. This factored a slow-down in the oil business production activity in the Gulf of Mexico throughout this American region, but the oil industry sometimes has a way of putting themselves back in production. Therefore the Gulf of Mexico within these international waters of the United States is part of some people's place of work that have been damaged, including a vast amount of these people's homes that they reside in outside of work. This even forced a vast amount of people to leave that American Gulf States region to truly have a responsible life.

Homes, schools, hospitals, church's, businesses, and government offices considering the vast amounts of assets that where damaged during this 2005 hurricane is the factual problem within the partly insured recovery. The U.S. President George Bush declared the region a Disaster Area with an appropriate state of Emergency for assisting the observed conditions of those regional areas. Assessments of "damage" is, and became a very important fact about the cleanup from a hurricane, and or more so the flooding. This assessment process most times includes the factors within insurance compensation payments, and most all levels of government operating cost that provides an equation to solve factual problems with solutions.

These problems of a catastrophic capacity consisted of various dangerous levels of contamination that where submerged in the flood waters consisting of things such as oil, paint, and other poisonous contaminates. Some problems would also include the regional dogs, cats, rats, poisonous snakes, reptile alligators, and other habitants. Observing these factors, it was very important that young children must be severely guided, and closely supervised by their parents or other's during this disaster, and the process of cleaning including asset recovery. Some elderly people truly had a hard time surviving without productive young people of concern. In addition within this hurricane (Katrina) during 2005 it had a storm after mass which consisted of vast amounts of dead people, and animal body remains that where compounded in the devastating flood waters. This sustained problem that existed for weeks with increased levels of contaminated water was tremendous until cleanup and people where accounted for as deceased, or living.

Upon this catastrophic disaster, and concern over 1,500 people died in the flood waters. A vast amount of animals (dead or alive) where removed from the contaminated water, and subdued wet lands. This also included various household, and commercial chemical products that modified this diversified process of massive insurance claims with many different types of illnesses. In addition the consolidated factors of future evaluations is a duty, and priority that will have to be governed, and managed by various involved professionals, business priorities, and citizens. Upon this disaster even the concern of the local police, and fire department officials had to stabilize people stilling from different retail stores to get what they needed, and wanted considering this offered additional problems, and losses (c/o some insured) that where hard, and complex to avoid. This therefore was observed, and considered as a total restriction of life with non-livable standards from the disaster that had occurred. Observing the evaluation of this massive problem in America, this is the considered fact of a consolidated problem to be the total concept within a disaster.

Another factor within this terrible hurricane Katrina disaster that also caused suffering was a loss of government assets, and most logical communication systems. During most storms of this capacity occasionally telephone systems may possibly work, but when utility towers, and telephone cables are "damaged", this destroys that operating system, and the format of people making contact, and talking to other people on telephones. Considering this, most factors within government communication, and various official duties, which included the loss of New Orleans police department officials, all social, and governed conditions became another worrisome factor. In addition to police, and fire department officials not able to maintain complete order, different levels of government still had emergency step by step duties. The hurricane Katrina caused problems to all electrical power which had been blacked out with no time consideration of when the public utilities would be restored. Considering this problem of working in the dark of the night to rescue stranded people, most efforts became complex for everyone in New Orleans.

This array of problems following the hurricane also includes the duties within what it takes for people to be rushed to the nearest hospitals of appropriate operating capacity to have safe, and responsible health care matters diagnosed, and treated. These professional service issues are relevant in certain hospital facilities that survived most all aspects of the storm, and hurricane. It's no doubt that this was one of the worse "government, and engineering" disasters of our American society, and times of today, "due to obsolete" water retention levees. Although "Mother Nature" is not an easy one to control, this therefore consisted of the consideration that the American society (c/o New Orleans) could have done better to prevent, and be prepared for this issue. This severely includes the disaster within insurance business repercussions.

The hospital's, and other businesses also consist of insurance concerns that appropriated their operating capacity of liability. Observing the format of liabilities that are required to work with the local, counties, states, and even the federal government officials being relevant disciplines, these people with duties were subjected to the most extreme conditions to provide security, and efficient control. The discipline, and factor of ethics consisting of U.S. Anti-Trust laws of equality including minority contractor issues (c/o no-bid contracts) where considered, and this was observed to coordinate any local contractors that could be helpful. This also factored issues within the format that professional government contractors where needed and considered after "law, and order" was reestablished.

Observing these factors of logic within Hurricane Katrina, this means the complex amount of cost that remained, and with workable duties would be completely understood, but all other concerns of a well-developed society with this disaster had to be evaluated. Considering this financial, and contractual business issue it included certain Architecture, Engineering, and Construction contractors from Louisiana (c/o New Orleans), and other different parts of America. A valid concern is that they would have to comply with the U.S. individual states, and federal Constitutional laws although special amendments from government where applied. This was vital to get hospitals, paramedics, police, and fire department officials back in operating order. Therefore mandates to restore the "New Orleans Metropolitan Area" was set on an agenda, but it's an agenda with conditional government legislative amendments that will take years, and even decades for certain levels of a full recovery.

When an individual as well as an insurance company official looks, and reviews the cost of a business, and even people subjected to medical procedures of a hospital, it consist of things such as the expenses of a critical medical operation. A normal medical operation of internal medicine procedures will consist of an hour or more of professional liabilities (diverting light, water, oxygen fixtures, and other equipment on and off) with certain equipment, special nurse assistance procedures, and different medications. Sometimes these are multiple operations at one time. Also this includes a vast amount of special tools, and materials that the professional medical surgeon requires for a successful surgery in an operating room environment. Hospital disciplines, just like other businesses, and even some hobbies that require special procedures, or tools, and ways within conducting professional procedures must be done right. Observing this professional procedure is part of making this the consideration of partial duties of most all professional disciplines of liability workable. Therefore as Americans within business markets, and certain liability's we must be careful to provide professions, and occupations these concerned factors which become the regular standards of good, and bad lawful decisions.

Another problem, and debated concern was the vast amount of inventory that was damaged during this (2005) hurricane Katrina that included cars, and trucks that where located at a vast amount of automobile dealerships. This conditional concern includes massive amounts of vehicles that where owned by the metropolitan issues of government, businesses, the people of New Orleans, and of other city, town, and state constituents. Within this combination of vehicle asset claims, there was hundreds of thousands of vehicles destroyed, or damaged severely, and this factor, and cost had many good, and bad insured variations. Only a certain amount of automobile dealerships, and other businesses restructured before most individual citizen's, and some smaller businesses. This was the business diversion apart from those that relocated or closed after the disasters of hurricane Katrina. Another factor includes their small, or large capacity of inventory that could not be saved, and this compiled factual financial losses. Some things within products or inventory are insured, and some item's, and things are not. This factual cost was vital to consolidate within the awareness to continue the balance of most all business bookkeeping in the American Gulf States that consist of present, and future business concerns.

Contrary to the insurance business factors within conducting the duties of certain business operations, this recovery process was becoming complex considering how the government and public, private businesses had to work together. This was observed when the levees of the City of New Orleans collapsed, and the flood water capacities became rational. These levees where built as government assets to protect the citizens, and society which means the maintenance with vital upgrades of this floodwall system was ignored. This lack of governed awareness destroyed the safety, and liability of the people. The flood waters caused most of these damages, and this means our American society of engineering, and government has severe problems that need fixing. Some, or most of the people of Louisiana should hope that Mayor Ray Nagan, and others have learned from this disaster. The actual wind and rain from the hurricane was one factor, but the flood waters from the levee system that collapsed is what caused these human fatal, and property damage issues at various historical rates.

Throughout the United States, and the many geographical regions of our American industry of insurance companies, and the businesses including various households that have been hit with record amounts of damage, most all have hopes that these claims can be adjusted, and compensated. So, observing various recent historical disasters this has accumulated financial damages to businesses, and the property people own at some of the worse means possible. Earthquakes are one of the many bad conditions with damages especially in states like California, and it's geographic atmosphere. During the late 1990s, and the early 2000s, mudslides, and forest wildfires became another catastrophic problem in California, and a few other western states. These geographical, social, and financial concerns consisted of some insurance companies, and the people which found these issues to be vitally observant to maintain relevant issues about prevention, and or protecting their property. As it applies to insurance, and personal business matter's these problems carried a high rate of damage, and various rates of policy insurance values.

The logic of making adjustments to manage most concerns of damage are complex values to the effective needs of protection, and possible compensation within the various detailed types of possible regional disasters. These disasters that occurred in California most times consisted of workable liabilities to be reviewed. This is a vital concern, and consideration about the coverage of claims (c/o adjustments) that had to be appropriately understood, factored, and applied with various adjusted clams, and preventative issues with prepared future levels of caution. These catastrophic disasters, and other un-formatted issues, including the format of liability within the different types of insurance concerns had discretionary, or contingent factors such as mudslides with clams, and wildfire clam's. Clams such as these where newly becoming a conflict because the geological settings where changing tremendously with new construction, and how it coordinated the effect upon financial protection to compensate settlements for these damages. Once the forest wildfire would destroy a majority of trees, then the unattended soil was left soft, and then continued to accumulate rainwater increasing ground conditions to break apart causing mudslide conditions which was another contingent problem that becomes a conditional disaster. This observation concerning geographic, and development conditions within the West Coast Region of the United States was complex for some people due to the fact that sometimes an earthquake is expected, but mudslides, or forest wildfires near residential areas became the most serious problem based on contingent liabilities. Therefore changing, or upgrading the geological ground components of sub-grade conditions especially in the mountains, is considered a challenge to the solemn state of various people's community of living.

The California mudslides became a very complex liability with severe ground conditions of danger for house's, and road's that where built in the mountains. Observing these mudslides from the higher elevations of the mountains, some houses moved from one location "downward" to another due to massive flowing wet mud. This also eliminated, and destroyed certain roads, and the property lots that certain expensive houses were built on. Some very expensive house's where still under construction that had none, or incomplete insurance coverage. Considering these houses in the mountains, certain California, and Arizona debates, and professional arguments existed about building so many houses in the mountains. Another issue was the congested amount of houses that were taking up space on mountains which some people acknowledged that this disturbs wildlife, and the preservation of natural values. This vital debate consisted of a few other vital professional factors which had to be considered, and that's the control of geographic sub-grade conditions which are unpredictable within mud, and rain applicable with the concern of earthquakes. Considering this combination of natural beauty in the mountains, and these occasionally unpredictable disasters, this conflict stricken region of value throughout the West Coast, and it's scientific conditions becomes complex to predict, but some geological problems could have been observed "preventively".

Considering the liabilities within American business markets with certain geological and engineering studies of research, these evaluation issues become important to consolidate predictions of financial claims, and policy issues of insurance. This becomes the format of business that Scientific Professional's pursue as a format of business procedures, and that is consistent with most applicable insurance, engineering, and even construction business considerations of effective liabilities. Then these factors of general living standards become important evaluated estimates, and predictions. A good professional evaluation provides the lowest level, to the highest level of contingent liability problems possible, but the lower the contingent risk is, the better things are considered. Upon understanding the different levels of contingencies in our American society of business, these are financial management observed duties applied to everything that could happen unexpectedly. This issued format of planning, and sacrifices is a vital factor for all people that work to achieve a formal good life. Therefore within managing a home, business, organization, or even a government office with all lawful liabilities, and contingent factors, this is how we overcome most problems with the best professional solutions possible.

Most all businesses, industries, and occasionally government consisting of vital market liability duties, and effort have manageable concerns to work to observe procurements that these assets are considered for with most contingent liabilities. These become the things that are to be taken very serious with most levels of caution. The American automobile industry and the major oil companies of the U.S.A. are logical examples that include oil spills, or vehicle parts that malfunction. Occasionally there is also "pharmaceutical products" that consist of good and bad problems with contingent factors that must be reviewed by law, observed within clinical studies, and understood by industry professionals. Insurance companies, and banking establishments are considered some of the businesses with the highest level of contingent disciplines, and that's why when the American economy is doing good they factor a particular kind of growth, and or stability. Some companies including banks, and insurance agency businesses have suffered failure due to a lack of contingent factors considering some of their disputes to hold on to business may have been with different conditions from failing banks. The conditions of these contingent facts in our American society can be the loss of liability, and liquidity that consist of people's day by day survival. This therefore is a factually important subject within most all companies progress within business conditions of liability, and ethical discipline.

American International Group Inc. (AIG), and some other large American insurance companies where effected with contingent financial losses after the September 11, 2001 terrorist attacks. These contingent base losses from AIG amounted to about $500 to $800 million dollars. These, and a few factual subjects such as insuring investment brokerage firms has lead AIG Inc. into the resource of asking the United States government for a financial bailout consideration. Observing the September 11, 2001 attacks various American insurance businesses loss more than an estimated $50 billion dollars. These are the types of similar losses that where suffered, and or compounded from the hurricane Katrina, but the hurricane disaster consisted of more uninsured people, and probably some under-insured, and uninsured businesses. Upon these issues within the American system of government that takes a vast amount of concern for the people, and businesses when most all parts of America's general welfare is threatened, this therefore has duties that require vital conditions of effort. This factor within the general public consist of problem's that contingently effect the poorest people, to the wealthiest of people, and most all "residentially started" businesses, and corporations.

Observing the different company's such as the General Electric Corporation, and American International Group Incorporated whom suffered hard times after September 11, 2001 this gave cause to the General Electric Corporation to consider the sale of its commercial insurance business. General Electric Corporation made these evaluated decisions possibly due to the massive losses in the insurance markets within business, and a lack of industry standards (c/o large ticket finance protection) within the terrorist (9-11 Report) attacks. These economic nerve stricken liabilities also included a vast amount of manufacturing plant explosions not at General Electric, but other comparable manufactures with massive equipment operations, and liability concerns. These plant explosions destroyed expensive equipment, with certain people injured (causing fatality & liquidity concerns), and then this imposed accumulated cost to most all business constituents involved. This dose become similar to the cost, and liability insured values of "even" products like GE jet engines that are manufactured for a vast amount of commercial airplanes. This jet engine business concern can be a negative financial conflict due to the economic trouble of the airline industry. Therefore besides 1995, the years of 2001 to 2006 have accumulated very expensive levels of personal, and business expense damage's with conflicting adjustments in most financial, and business product markets which a vast amount of businesses, and people have been effected.

Considering our American markets that consist of these certain prosperous business matters apart from terrorism, and other disasters, this observation of good, and more so bad years of economic conditions usually require the appropriate need of good business, and government decision making. Various conflicts convinced the State Farm Insurance Company during 2003, and 2004 observing the economic, and financial losses of 2001 to decide to sale their new homeowner's insurance policy business. This homeowner's insurance business and concern was, and is in some capacity an issue that continues to be a vital business concern. One good, or interesting point is that Edward Rust Sr. has been a stable CEO of State Farm Insurance Company for over 25 years which means he knows the business.

Another State Farm Insurance issue is observed that at various times their business was productively important in 20 different states as it applies to home, and even auto insurance which they still provide various policies for in some concerns. State Farm, and other insurance companies have loss heavily during the 1990s when certain subdivisions of new houses in Illinois suffered from massive tornado's that destroyed newly built houses, and other assets in certain subdivisions. This problem occurred over and over again even with severe flood damages in various other states. These factors of damage increased State Farm insurance clam payments which then suffered along with a failing mortgage market with less people having, and or needing the concern of buying homeowners insurance. Observing the State Farm Insurance Company, at one time operating productively in the United States upon which this company conditionally witnessed, and endured high levels of claims for damages, now their company has changed. The State Farm Insurance Co eliminated the offering of their stock purchasing opportunities, and this became another loss of liquidity.

The Midwest of the United States suffered different problems within liability, and earnings considering certain steel mill commercial facility gas explosions. In Northwest Indiana corporate businesses such as U.S. Steel, Bethlehem Steel, Inland Steel, and Bata Steel all suffered this problem on occasions in the 1990s with Bata Steel suffering the worse explosion. In addition unproductive insurance contingencies also had a calculated effect from some residential gas explosions, tornado's (c/o structures), and fires which was a severe set-back for many household families, and even businesses. None of these concerns "residentially" seem to be as bad as the September 2010 gas explosion in San Bruno, California upon which Pacific Gas & Electric did not seem to keep certain sub-grade gas pipes upgraded, even with the appropriate economic funding. This explosion killed 4 people, and destroyed about 40 neighborhood house's.

Considering other contingencies, vast amounts of households where effected by issues that included various criminal damages, seasonal and conflicting automobile accidents with certain other problems. Also other contingencies consisted of numerous states which have suffered similar residential and more so commercial explosion's that is a conflicting problem that seems to be headed out of some factual control. These were problems that cost a vast amount of insurance company's money, outlining various businesses with faults. Then this occasionally caused clients there solitude, domestic tranquility, and the concern that our American society of Engineering, and certain related occupations has needs of severe improvements. Some people would imply throughout various states that from certain insurance business conflicts compared to the rate of auto accidents in some regions, gave cause that the vehicle junk yards have gained more than some insurance businesses.

Throughout these economic times of conflict including the Prudential Insurance Incorporated business whom sold its auto, and home insurance business operation to the Liberty Mutual Insurance Group and Palisades Safety and Insurance Association for $673 million dollars, this becomes evident that certain prosperous liability issues did not come easy. This was a major adjustment with some insurance business concerns including the fact that the Prudential Insurance provider in the Midwest of the United States had similar problems which occurred at the State Farm Insurance Company whom suffered liquidity problems, and sold a money-losing insurance division for new home policies. Other insurance companies are starting to reorganize certain issues that include the concept of becoming a financial service provider such as within the Hartford Insurance Co., and the Hartford Financial Services Group. This is similar to the Prudential Insurance Company, and even some conditions at the State Farm Insurance Company, which has established a "financial service business company" or group maybe to readjust from losses. Observing the American society of businesses, and insurance company's it is very important that we understand the best values of anti-trust related sectors of individual business success, and expansion. Then business survival or success can exist for some businesses without needing to enter into the banking related industries.

Some of these business decisions were made before the September 11, 2001 terrorist attacks which added additional concerns. The consideration of business decisions that occurred after the terrorist attacks also became factored with hurricane Katrina, and thousands of other issued conflicts. The American financial markets have been affected with some good, but more so bad out comes that put the American economy, and people in a conditional state of complicated matters with these tragedies. Understanding this, large businesses, and government including insurance company's may have regretted some of these very expensive hard working investments into other conglomerate market industries of business. These are the factors that are becoming a financial hardship to certain business customers, clients, and their own business ownership values observing the 2007 thru 2010 financial, and asset losses that is effecting many different regions of America.

During the years of 2007, and 2008, a vast amount of financial service companies are accumulating major losses in the mortgage lending, and insurance markets. This concept of diversified losses has also been part of some good, and bad times for insurance companies that occasionally, or vitally depend on certain financial service businesses, and companies. Warren Buffet, and his company Berkshire Hathaway during the first quarter of 2008 has earned money as a successful insurance company. While operating Berkshire Hathaway, Warren Buffet has also managed a large portfolio of investments within some losses lately in an international, and United States domestic capacity. His insurance company Berkshire Hathaway also consist of a shrewd public (c/o common and preferred) stock offering price, and this is evident with a large principal cost (thousands; to tens of thousands of dollars) for each share of stock, and this maintains the balance of liquidity, and not so much for "small or uncommitted investor" opportunities.

Merrill Lynch investments during the last two quarters of 2007, and the beginning of 2008 have suffered losses above $8 billion dollars. These losses were due to a complex housing, and lending market that has expanded with unproductive business practices. Stanley O'Neal was removed as Merrill Lynch's Chief Executive Officer just like a few other CEO's that have suffered these bad financial times, and market conditions within other investment companies, various banks, and a vast amount of insurance company's. Considering Stanley O'Neal whom retired after this sad factor of business market concerns he will receive more than $100 million dollars of retirement pay, and these corporate financial problems at Merrill Lynch will require long-term decision making that is productive, and lawful by the company. Some of these financial and economic losses consisted of similar problems within numerous brokerage firms (c/o Merrill Lynch, Goldman Sachs, and various others) that AIG Inc. sold insurance to, and for certain investment items of agreement that these investment brokers offered. In so many words we are lead to ask did AIG, and maybe another try to insure the additional deposit matters that the FDIC dose not insure in the overall banking industry? This observation concludes (c/o 2007 to 2009) that these investment losses with some insurance conflicts are affecting all types of small and large investors, and various critical businesses in America.

Within my opinion this array of insurance, and financial issues is similar to some other liability concerns which includes mergers, and issues of conglomerate business activities that are leading the American economy into very complex times. Corporate mergers or people buying other American people's businesses is not totally destructive, but when restructuring a business, or a newly merged management the law's, and other business disciplines, and decision making become vital including the resources of people, and taxable economic earnings. Observing these conflicts this means that a vital issue of local or regular banking businesses with insurance concerns will, or may have a hard time making (profitable) money as a "commerce or investment" bank. The American financial brokerage service businesses will, or may have a hard time making (profitable) money as an investment bank business, but the logic of insuring brokerage products or services will take conditional decision making just like most all expanding businesses. Then we have insurance companies that may depend on these other industries, and therefore the insurance companies may have a hard time making profits, or money as good insurance companies, and businesses. The American society of people, businesses, and even government depend on various insurance companies, and businesses including them, and other public, or private businesses. Then there is a need to do their part as good corporate, or business citizens, and constituents.

American Food, Pharmaceutical,
& Business Liabilities
(9)

CHAPTER NINE
(9)

The United States Library of Congress

American Food, Pharmaceutical, & Business Liabilities
(9)

Throughout the American society there is vital food, and pharmaceutical business liability issues that become relatively important to the people of the United States, and other countries. This becomes a combination of health concerned issues throughout America. These markets of the United States within agriculture commodities consist of liability factors within the supply of food, and pharmaceutical drug products to the American society. Understanding these vital, and appropriate necessities become vital factors upon which people, and even their pet animals depend on to live, and all to maintain good health. Observing these concerns that occasionally can be determined as life or death or more so Pubic Health law issues the United States government established the United States Food and Drug Administration (FDA) to coordinate the best methods within food, and drug products with diverse medical services. Understanding the duties of the Food and Drug Administration of the United States Department of Health, Education, and Welfare they consist of an evaluation process on all food, and pharmaceutical drug products that are offered, and sold to the American society of people, and developing products within manufacturing processes.

Most food and pharmaceutical companies in America consist of products with complex or logical ingredients that company's and corporations spend time researching, and developing within manufacturing processes. These businesses usually consist of a strong concept of corporate liquidity to value the cost of these important procedures, discoveries, and sale's that usually improve. Some of the American pharmaceutical company's today with disciplines of research consist of Pfizer Inc., Merck & Company, Eli Lilly & Company, Abbott Laboratories, Johnson & Johnson Inc, Baxter International, and others that have future potential. These consolidated businesses (c/o some universities) doing research on products for the general public are then reviewed by the U.S. Food and Drug Administration. These United States government procedures also consist of the FDA conducting additional research with clinical and testimonial evidence in hearings to approve new medicines, and the review of other products that may then be questionable within liability. Observing this internal medicine approval process, these levels of evaluation give the U.S. government's approval within the safety, and effectiveness of medicine, and various resources of disciplined medical procedures. Understanding this concern, the FDA was established to enforce the Food, Drug, and Cosmetic Act which has a concern for any products that could have harmful effects, and how they are offered to citizen / patients of the American general public. These liability concerns to protect the health of American citizens become an issue for the many products that various companies make as food, drugs, and or cosmetics.

The American market for food products over the last 50 to 100 years has went through many different changes. A few of the largest American food company's (c/o beverage company's) are Kraft Foods, ConAgra Foods, Kroger, Monsanto, Coca Cola, PepsiCo, Kellogg Company, and Tyson Foods. Considering this understanding, some of the most productively expanding businesses and corporations consist of liquidity values, and issues that must be pursued with careful evaluation. For hundreds of years Americans have found, and created medicine products that help solve medical problems, and food to feed the people so that they can live with good rates of nutrition, which is becoming a resource of liability. Over the years these products have went through the conditional format of good, bad, and conflicting improvements, or a process of lawful elimination. This becomes the modification process of food and pharmaceutical items that hopefully don't make people severely sick, and or with additional illness conditions. The moderation, and procedures of shipping, content of food ingredients, and now the relevant good health of farm raised animals are consistent with all parts of this step by step market, and liability process. Understanding this variation of commodities is the life line of the American food, beverages, and the medical industry, which all includes business, and logical cost to its many consumers within customers.

Within the "American Markets of Pharmaceutical" products, a vast amount of over-the-counter drugs, and pharmaceutical prescribed drug products have had to endure the changing times of America. Just like food companies, the pharmaceutical companies have had to bring in good products, and then take out certain bad products which may be part of a lawsuit, or a United States major health concern. This evaluation process is a liability issue of argumentative conditions by the company that develops, and manufactures the best products possible, and what health or food conditions it will improve. This is also applicable to the administered duties of the FDA for the regulated purity of food, the effectiveness of medicines, and various therapeutic devices. It is just as important in this legal format to the FDA that these products have truthfulness within labels, and the safety with honesty of packaging. Understanding packaging, and distribution of medicines from various pharmaceutical companies during 2007, they provided doctor's offices with more than 240,000,350 samples of medicine with a value of more than $3.26 billion dollars to market their products. These are usually considered their best products upon which they sale large volumes of medicine to the medical industry throughout the vast amount of communities in America. Therefore, there is a level of confidence that "most, but not all" of these medical products are workable with high rates of liability.

Observing doctors, and patient's that consist of good, and occasional bad medical products that don't do good, this can cause a severe effect to businesses, professionals, various people, and certain values of the market. Throughout the American food supply of products this also becomes a problem when food products are not cared for properly with various process procedures. It is relevant to say, and understand that various exquisite restaurants, and grocery stores that can provide excellent food products, and services for preparing meals can be affected by this problem, if they are not careful. Even drug stores with a small or large volume of store locations, and customers must maintain a format of liability including the resource of choosing some non-prescription medication items that are the best logical products. Contrary to this market issue, this becomes a matter of business owners that choose the best or most logical products they can offer. This also consist of the short term, or long term complaints from customers that must be evaluated. Considering large retail drug stores like Walgreen's Co., Osco Drug's, CVS Caremark Corp. and grocery stores like Safeway similar to restaurants like McDonalds, Burger King, Red Lobster and a few others, they have liability, and customer satisfaction managing disciplines that distinctively apply. These corporate businesses stress these values that go along the resource of their established business plan for all employees. Sometimes this cost of the best items is part of a market discipline within managing, and maintaining potential earnings, and the volume of effective customers to keep a productive establishment within a business setting.

American farmers, farm businesses, and certain diversified farmers from other parts of the world have produced so many food products at high volume rates that they donate reserve amounts as subsidized food to certain needy or distressed organizations, countries, or regions. Certain medicines are also provided within similar concerns. The U.S. government and other countries have great appreciation for this process of donations. Also this is workable with the United Nations to appropriate standards of good foreign relations. This becomes a tax deductible item upon which their farm product sale's, and business activity can be stabilized with lower tax payments if the farm is a productive resource. Between the 1930s, and 2009 there has been a loss of about 5 million farm's; leaving about 2 million that operated as production farm businesses in some cases as household farms in America. Therefore the resource of American non-durable commodities and live-stock has changed with bigger farms, and the managing of most farm resources. Another business consideration is that a farm business is just like a vast amount of other new and old business sectors in America, upon were commitments, and sacrifices become important just like the existing laws, and social factors of society.

The logic of farming in America is still on occasions a resource of the mom, pop, and family traditional farm business processes, but some conditions have changed to consist of complete farm business operations. These conditions exist where production, and liability is a second nature to prepare for the development, and manufacture of pharmaceutical, and food products throughout America. An exception to mid-west family farms, and the loss of millions of farm's over the decades, the United States has observed corporate or factory farms develop into enormous operations. These farm's produce crop commodities at larger rates than most traditional farm's ever have. This includes how they can now feed animal's, and maintain commodities such as dairy products from hundreds of cows, hogs, chickens, or other live-stock on a daily factory format of farm processes, and logical procedures.

Considering the American mid-west regions of Indiana, Illinois, Iowa, and Ohio which are large corn producing states, it should be understood that corn commodities can be used for many purposes similar to wheat, fertilizer, and soybean. Corn being one of the most diverse farming commodity's, it produces cornstarch, corn syrup, corn flakes, corn oil, and ethanol fuel including the vast amount of corn vegetable products that people eat with various meals. Also these state's provide corn products to almost every part of America, and different parts of the world, and this requires workable decisions. This becomes the logical values within markets, and business that requires managing small, and large business issues of liquidity, and earnings. Also these and a few other states grow, and produce wheat, soybean, and raise live-stock which is a vital combination, and part of both American food, and pharmaceutical markets of liability for non-durable products, and bi-products.

The southeast and the southwest of the United States consist of similar farming capacities of fruits such as oranges, peaches, cherry's, and grapes. California leads the nation (c/o America) in grapes, but is second (2nd) to only Florida in producing oranges. Texas, and Nebraska are the major production leaders in the American industry of beef cattle product's. Wisconsin, and Minnesota are the American major producers of dairy cattle products such as milk, and cheese. These become some of the farm industrial production processes of food items that the United States Department of Agriculture (USDA) provides their seal of quality with inspections for, and this is usually considered as a high grade of quality. This keeps American farming and its base of consumers within logical markets that value most resources of liabilities within public, private businesses, and government within "all" making the best efforts in all levels of determination.

Another issue within the liability resource of products, come from the ocean, and other waterway's such as large lakes, rivers, and oceans similar to the Gulf of Mexico, and it's composites of scientific, and commodity values. The British Petroleum Company

(BP) at this time during 2010 has caused one of the worse issues of liability against the fishing industry of America with a massive oil well leaking out of control in the Gulf of Mexico. Apart from the farm land issues of soil contamination in some south-west oil producing regions, the coastal waters of Louisiana, Mississippi, and Alaska supply the highest rate of ocean wildlife products. The New Orleans fishing industry during 2009 before the oil well leak of 2010 was valued at about $2.1 billion dollars a year, and due to this accident various people in the fishing industry with others were hired by the BP Company to help the clean-up. For a substantial amount of time (c/o months or more) the Louisiana fishing concern has been lawfully put on hold, which consist of everyday being a loss of income to all working in the Gulf Coast fishing industry. These become the factors of where mostly American scientist and geologist make some of their most critical studies, or investigative evaluations of how some food, and ocean life scientific commodities have been affected environmentally. This also becomes the basic standard of evaluations within research to establish various medicines

The Alaskan Bay is part of a shipping harbor with various import / export products, and more so oil tanker shipping businesses with government, and market regulated issues. Contrary to this fact it relatively also consisted of American values within an enormous amount of fishing industry, and wildlife concerns where some effects from past oil spills linger. Upon this concern the food industry within seafood from Alaska is making a logical return with only slightly considered conflicts due to other industry matters. In March of 1989 the Exxon Valdez accidentally (with negligence) loss 12 million gallons of crude oil into these Alaskan Bay waters of America, and this gave that regions seafood industry a relevant concern. This critically hurt, and killed a vast amount of the environments sea life animals, and caused damage to certain levels of the fishing industry. Upon these issues, the American society has a vital liability to protect all soil, and waterway conditions to continue to produce these various important commodities, and even be consistent with its scientific specimens.

Every American market of food or pharmaceutical products with a non-durable natural production capacity of output depends on commodities for food, and chemical safety, and usage concerns can be affected by polluted conditions of nature. This consist of moat all natural commodities. There vital conditions of various natural process resources of nature, have a format of growth, and scientific disciplines that they work or struggle to appropriate in most of our established industry needs. When and if those conditions of nature are disturbed in terms of water, land, and air pollution or development, a vast amount of future concerns within potential problems must be considered, and evaluated.

From oil, and gas spills in Texas, and Oklahoma on land, various chemical plant explosions "contaminating' the air is also an occasional environmental health problem of concern. These factors also consist of a problem that exist in the compounds of oil, and other chemical's in the water which has given the United States, and corporations disastrous environmental attention of governed concern. Observing this social / industrial, and medical conflict vast amounts of industrial plants in Northwest Indiana (c/o U.S. Steel and various others) caused severe air, soil, and more so contamination problems to Lake Michigan. This industry chemical contamination process was killing certain various types of fish, and wildlife in Lake Michigan during the 1950s, and 1960s. The United States Environmental Protection Agency observes, and pursues these problems which are occasionally considered by the U.S. Food, and Drug Administration's format of clinical trials.

During the 1970s U.S. Steel and a few others became a major enforcement concern of the U.S. Environmental Protection Agency (EPA) to stop the pollution. Then U.S. Steel Corporation upon others were ordered to have responsibility for what they had polluted. This environmental problem left a variation of Gary, and Northwest Indiana citizens with occasional health problems observing the increasing water, and air pollution within certain places throughout the surroundings of the city of Gary. Over the years this problem near U.S. Steel (Gary Works) was cleaned up on the Lake Michigan shoreline with only wastewater, and soil contamination issues remaining during 2009. Whiting, Indiana is the site of (c/o Amoco Oil) British Petroleum Company, and Lever Bothers soap (c/o chemicals) which also contributed to some of these environmental conflicts. Considerably, even now a vast amount of dead fish are gone from the Lake Michigan shores of sandy beaches. These become issues of negligence, or sometimes corporate criminal offences (c/o others like *BP-Amoco Oil, *Mittal-Inland & Bethlehem Steel) upon which the corporate constituents, and even sometimes with government have not pursued some of their duties to the best of their abilities, or resources.

Between 2005 and 2007 more than 5 serious chemical plant explosions released very dangerous toxics into the air that also may have caused a problem to regional air supply values, and certain waterways. Some toxic explosions sent chemicals floating heavily into the air, and then settled (c/o acid and particle rain) into nearby waterways, and on certain composites of land. These types of explosions with fire, and even chemicals which consisted of toxics (c/o parts per billion) forced its way into other factories. This dangerous chemical toxic polluting the air within neighboring ventilation processes to supply the internal air flow for various other commercial, and even some residential facilities can provide medical problems of chocking and breathing. This is where more pharmaceutical products such as oxygen become important in various medical emergencies. These issues of certain industrial based commerce concerns are carefully observed, and reviewed for any potential hazards of liability to other products, and people in the general area. In some zoning requirements that exist in the regulatory parameters of most city, and town government's, a logical understanding is usually observed for (commercial & residential) proximity state, and federal laws within safety, and sometimes importantly "scientific principals". In reference of American Environmental Law's, these disciplines where established as doing business with the best possible solutions, and methods.

To observe chemical explosions with toxic problems, the year 2007 was tremendously bad. The Chemcentral Corporation of Kansas City, Missouri had a chemical plant explosion that left a large cloud of toxic black smoke throughout the entire metropolitan downtown area of Kansas City, Mo. This type of chemical smoke with toxics leaving black stains, and contaminated ashes that becomes a factual hazard consisted of a "vital must" to be considered for logical clean up. Understanding the severe magnitude of the explosion this was a tremendous problem although no one was killed during the explosive impact. It also causes a liability problem to surrounding industries, but the main liability was left with Chemcentral Corp. To truly observe this problem in America, there has been to many chemical explosions during the first decade of 2000, and the people are paying an even bigger cost with a bad economy, and environmental damage! As pharmaceutical, and food manufactures are concerned, their chemical process procedures don't seem to be the worse, but there has been danger in some of these process facilities. Therefore whatever type of manufacturing process that is continuous including gas, electrical, and a vast amount of non-durable commodity products has manufacturing issues of caution that always needs to be exercised.

A food production process at ConAgra Foods Inc. in Garner, North Carolina (c/o 2007) suffered a massive explosion where 2 people died, and 3 others were missing. This explosion caused damage to various parts of the large manufacturing facilities roof structure, and walls. ConAgra Foods Inc. is a large productive food processing business, but the issue of worker's, and professionals at this company and others must consider the liability responsibilities of safety that they must uphold. Besides others like in Morganton, N.C. the Synthron Inc. (2006) chemical plant explosion with soil, and air contamination became another observed potential problem due to chemicals that are released onto the land. Within the Texas City, Texas BP Company (2005) fatal chemical plant explosion which is part of another chemical, and commodity process facility with contamination, these issues become an overall threat to the industry, and social values of society. These plant explosions and other issues within the American society cause a vast amount of people to have long term injuries, "if they survived". This became a strong commitment to pharmaceutical businesses, and the logical evaluation from doctor's to provide helpful services for these people that are injured. Most of the injured people will be suffering medical problems for years, and decades to come. Hospital emergency, and long-term care concern is part of these liability subjects with the market, and purchase of food, and medical items that must be reliably, and consistent to most all liable resources. Contrary to some of these damages any factual threat within issues are important to safety, and other concerns with proper work duties. These certain process procedures should not have been a problem, but the liability of the American medical industry is the next issue of dependable logic.

Within dangerous issues in society such as contamination or infection's including other health problem concerns, and issues the United States government has a discipline within the important uses, and requirements of vaccines. Harmful accident's is only a part of this enormous resource of concern. Everyone in the United States during childhood is required to have a set of vaccination shot's. This becomes a liability to prevent most all children, and people from severely dangerous diseases. A vaccine is administered for prevention, amelioration, or the treatment of infectious diseases. The American pharmaceutical companies with some other company's throughout other parts of the world observe that certain diseases have a tendency to cause harm to people, and even how these diseases can spread. Most of these diseases are influenza, measles, mumps, plaque, poliomyelitis, rabies, Rocky Mountain spotted fever, smallpox, tuberculosis, yellow fever, and a few others. Various American pharmaceutical companies manufacture different vaccine's for diseases such as Hepatitis, Chickenpox, Cancer, and others including the Flu. These corporations such as Merck & Company, Pfizer Incorporated, Ely Lilly & Company, and a few others develop various formulas, and this is followed by clinical trials, which usually demonstrates the benefits of their various determined medicines, and vaccines.

Hospitals throughout America consist of a vast amount of purchases (c/o billions of dollars) within food products, and medical supply's which vitally includes a vast amount of medicines. The American society of hospital's during this economic crisis before, and after the year 2000 have stumbled on some very tuff times due to the early 2000 millennium, and decade economy. With the requirement of medications, and more so vaccines considering a rising cost on the majority of products a vast amount of hospitals, and nursing homes have had to restructure, or "go out of business". On occasions this can be part of the overall liquidity problems of the American economy, and therefore evaluations with planning, and duties of good management may have only slightly prevented this problem. Considering this critical problem, hardly any food, or pharmaceutical businesses have suffered financially.

The concern, and consideration of how close some food companies, and pharmaceutical company's work together with hospitals observing the concept, and liability of business this consist of logical disciplines of supply, quality, and management that understands professionalism. This is the value of survival that is the discipline of workable management. Hospital's that have acquired severe financial problems seems conflicting mostly from problems that exist with government funds from a county government, and the state government within lately consisting of a budget crisis. The management of most all hospitals has the duty to make all work a productive commitment professionally, and the operating cost, liquidity, and profits that are managed upon achieving business goals. Also it has been considerably discussed that a vast amount of illegal aliens from mostly Mexico go to various hospitals, but most have no social security number, and way to pay certain bills for services. Indiana, Illinois, New Mexico, Texas, Arizona, California, and a few other states on the east coast such as Massachusetts, New York, and Florida have had hard times keeping a few hospitals open, and various medical clinic's from closing. This also becomes a concern in Florida with various Haitians, and Cubans coming to America illegally, but the Arizona, and Texas boarder issue is worse. Therefore even as nursing homes for the elderly, and severely ill people have been closing which outlines that, America has acquired the political or government decisions on what to do to help these people, while tapping an economic crisis.

Observing a majority of the changing atmosphere within businesses in America complacent management, and government with uninvolved employees looks to be the losing factor to the people, and the liability of a strong economy. As we observe food, pharmaceutical, oil, or even banking businesses the American society must improve their employed commitment to productive liabilities. The management, the labor unions, the non-union labor force, and anyone or everyone in the American workforce must recognize or be managed to understand what they do on the job will more than likely determine if their job or company will be around when they retire. This also includes whom, and how their children might be employed with concerning the future of the American society. This will apply to say if a company survives there is logic, but some with too many labor conflicts, or destructive issues of greed, these businesses have been factual to fail.

Considering most everything in the American society consist of a cost, a resource of economic values, and decisions will continue to be vitally important. The moderate cost within food, and internal medicine is a fraction of the industry values that keep America productive for the future. Upon this concern, and "factor" it is logical to say we need as many productive people, businesses, and corporations as possible providing issues of economic discipline, and prosperity to keep growing as a well-developed society. The logical concern even exist with the advancements of information technology, computer systems, wireless and satellite communication systems, and other concerned advancements throughout industry that is not to give destructive complacent thinking, and living. Otherwise the level of advanced technology should be productively safe without mental, physical, financial, and fatal harm to the people, and various assets within society. These issues include the health, and the wellbeing of the people that is part of this need within advancements that work along with productive solutions. Therefore to only keep the vitality of cleaning up from massive explosion's with contamination without fixing the problem, is a format of not having valued levels of occupations, professions, and especially markets which often push American standards backwards. This will keep bad food, and medical services from helping the people, and other problems of society including maybe the preventative resurgence of war. Then this becomes a severe problem that we the people will continue to see as a bad economy, unprofessional people, and American issues that cause depression.

Government, Business, Labor And Liabilities Within Markets
(10)

CHAPTER TEN
(10)

The United States Library of Congress

Government, Business, Labor And Liabilities Within Markets

(10)

The American society including the individual state governments and the United States federal government is the U.S. Constitutional formation of our well-developed society within lawfully factual markets, and disciplines of liability. Over the decades up to the year 2000 within establishing most markets, businesses, and how the subject of liabilities are applied is based on lawful, and responsible disciplines throughout various businesses. This applies to the American people, businesses, and government that have benefited with the discipline of working together in most U.S. Constitutionally considered good, and some bad issues within progress. These disciplines apply to every state government in America which has laws for the resources of how markets, business, labor, and liabilities are to be appropriated within taxable earnings. Considering the different state governments, and their geographical concept of regional commodities, and other things such as the lively hood of the people within heavy industry, this is a base of conditional priorities consisting of business, labor, and government. Therefore the United States federal government has applicable laws to govern all parts of the American society with the most liable, and lawful format of resourceful conditions of logic.

Every year and decade in the United States there has been a diversified issue of products, and services that creates a new resource of business with developing markets throughout America, and occasionally abroad. This is a factual format of careful, and disciplined arbitration just as the liability within different products, and services for certain vehicles, computers, telephones, and different services, or products of food are offered to the general public in business. Also these markets and business developments depend on raw materials that factor a business to consolidate the format of durable and non-durable goods for most mass production processes. The American market of non-durable goods consist of fruits, vegetables, and most agriculture farming produce that must be sold promptly, before certain items go bad. American goods that are not always consumed daily or weekly by the purchaser, such as within accommodating machinery, appliances, furniture, or hardware items which are considered durable goods, consist of longer time spans in a market retail business environment.

Following large cost item's, and products such as cars, trucks, and most homes, and the many different major and minor residential and commercial appliances ranks third as the biggest, and most vital durable good products. These durable items within most American business, and household markets are products valued within appropriated disciplines of liquidity, and liability. The new products, and services within the fast, but cautious moving markets of computer user products, and items is still slightly lower on the list of important durable goods, but they are moving fast in the ranking with some very important qualities. Also included in certain markets of diversified products are raw materials that consist of certain types of mining, farming, and forest materials. These materials in America are important within the preoperational by-product use within factories, mills, and other production processes. Some of the most common raw materials are coal, iron ore, petroleum, cotton, paper, and different animal hides. These things that make up an outlined process of materials, products, and the format of how some services are specified as valuable becomes part of a relevant concept of liability in business. Therefore this is within the consolidated small, and large industrial base of American businesses, and markets being relevant factors of diversified issues to be managed.

Year, after year these formal conditions of markets, and business industry factors occasionally improve for the better depending on the past, and present conditions of management decisions within a production business, or corporation. From the years of the 1940s, and 1950s management of various conditions of business, and industry have also consisted of labor conditions that include unions, and some non-union issues of importance. Labor unions within American business must be observed with consideration carefully due to the cost of manufacturing, and other issues to a business operation which occasionally consisted of vital good, and bad business production factors. As businesses within competitive markets try to advance yearly, observing their annual review of numbers, profits, and other important issues certain values such as the safety of workers becomes vitally important. These values within management of business including budget matters, and various duties consist of prosperity values that can gain solitude. Understanding this solitude these are some of the vital conditions that are occasionally overlooked by some labor unions. More importantly the labor unions address vital issues within maintaining safety liabilities (c/o some wage issues) that may have relevance within a management's cost of expenditures. The large concept of management in American corporations with labor, and even non-labor issues within business operations must come together, and work lawfully productive on these workable concerns of American business.

The format of American labor, and management relations should not destroy one, or more businesses, but it does occur lately more than the logic of efficient good business duties. This observation of negligent or intentional damage to American companies, are created occasionally because of disagreements between labor, and management that is distinctively a factual business problem throughout America. When these disagreements become an issue between the management, and a labor union this sometimes has to be consolidated, and observed with solutions. These subject's, and solutions become a formal and sometimes informal concern with lawfully aggressive conditions (c/o some workable & non-workable issues) that may consist of justice from the courts, and government.

Internal corporate relations was observed when the "UAW union members representing the Chrysler Corporation" workers fought, and received a large healthcare funding agreement from management. This business liquidity being managed by the union became a problem, and then the funded Chrysler Union went bankrupt. Non-workable conflicts like this and the American economic down fall is viewed on both sides occasionally with labor, and management agreements that harm the economic liability of the company. Contrary to the company, it even harms the market for steel, vehicles, and other products. Products, and services mostly in these factory environments, or even in the mining of natural commodities are clearly observed by labor for mostly safety and wage reasons on numerous occasions. The logic within this management, and labor subject becomes the two sided financial expense concern that must be acceptable to business. This is vital within the economic priority of a business, or a company's management that has appropriate operating standards at certain labor capacity rates.

Understanding these issues of how labor unions sometimes can effect most small, or large company's, this importantly must be observed that if there is no company, the labor union may not have reason to exist. During the 1990s apart from the 1950s, and 1960s it seems that one problem of American liability that has occurred is more international conflicts occur when unions, and a few others cross corporate, and socially complex foreign boundaries.

These complex issues on a foreign relations concern of labor, and or business, sometimes exceeds the U.S. Constitutional disciplines of our American society. Therefore all of these conflicts have a meaning that consist of resources which could be relevant within national security, and American vulnerability concerns that should be observed by all involved with logical awareness.

It seems important to observe these lawful security and business issues within the American labor unions whom are not always foreign relation experts. This surly includes the United States Constitutional disciplines that government must apply with, and enforce concerning important decisions that must be made. One of the relevant issues being very important for labor unions was the fact that some Americans lacked good decision making. This was a problem when mass production plants occasionally had seriously injured employees during accidents on the job without management taking full consideration, and effort to solve the overall problem. Most good labor unions, and their leadership would help to understand that this was a problem for the employee, and their families household. Therefore even the concept of American labor union leadership should be consistent with the American system of government in the United States. This is the value to maintain responsible markets, and the humble duty to value the long-term existence of the American household, and the diversified issues of business, and social factors throughout America.

Observing the long-term discipline of business, labor, and certain issues of liability, all people and professionals involved have duties to lawfully understand, and evaluate the company. The Ford Motor Company, General Motors Corporation, United States Steel Corporation, and General Electric Corporation are interesting examples that have achieved success within these good, and bad issues of business with labor unions. Their format of business that includes the mass production within products also includes markets, and management issues of labor that are lawfully important. Even small businesses, and company's apart from these large issues of a corporation have similar legal responsibilities when their company, or business may consist of an experience of growth, and successful expansion. Certain internet companies have experienced a certain type of productive growth over the years of the 1990s, and 2000. Contrary to internet business expansions that have been productive, it is important to understand how manufacturing has materialized, and this is a format of evaluated conditions of a business, and market process including other connected industries. Therefore within the United States this has consisted of the occasional growth of very few small companies which has become complex, and diversified with vital concerns for the future of America.

The real fact, and problem is that companies with large amounts of labor presents has taken a beating financially. This includes issues that occasionally effect various community school districts, and then businesses throughout the govern towns, and cities whom can suffer are evident upon having a hard time restructuring. General Electric Corporation has probably a smaller percentage of labor union members today then some steel, and vehicle manufacturing businesses. This complex issue is because of General Electric's diversified labor, and non-labor factors in American industry, and professionalism which occasionally includes the complexity of other countries. Then, a person can observe the Ford Motor company's presence upon establishment in the United States that includes the American union members of the United Auto Workers (UAW) which may have made mistakes along with some conditions of management. Considering these different markets, most of these businesses and organized labor have different business plans of success. Then the employees concerning various business operating plans must take observation, and apply these duties effectively considering all business issues are part of relevant business decisions. Understanding this becomes important within having too maintain cost, and overall earnings that must be positive, and productive. Economic disciplines are also a relevant business factor within progress of the lawful importance to establish any kind of lawful business earnings. This even includes labor unions that should understand with careful and vital consideration that the format of an established business from any type of the American market will include the better resource of product's, and or services

Comparing computers, major appliances, and products such as steel, plastics, paper, automobiles, boats, and even airplanes, these types of manufacturing items, and their companies are part of the changing times of American business, and markets. Certain people would consider the last important factor of innovation in the American steel manufacturing industry, and markets was during the 1950s when Bethlehem Steel Corporation built a new plant in Northwest Indiana. This means that the company, and the market for steel products where producing good rates of business returns to a certain extent. General Motors Corporation, and the Ford Motor Company where building plants, and manufacturing cars, and trucks at good rates, but they have seen labor strikes, foreign competition, and bad investments that cost them more then they earn. Another issue included the people that bought cars (c/o some housing) they could not afford during a bad American economy. Actually a vast amount of people retained ownership of new vehicles, also had accidents, and totaled the car leaving the insurance company, and the auto company to split the cost that became a severe problem of liquidity as well.

The considerable expansion in purchases, and the use of computers has established internet news collaborated mergers within company's such as "Microsoft Corporation, and National Broadcasting Corporation" with (NBC), and as (MSNBC). This subsidiary television cable programming has become MSNBC along with others as television programming with outlined internet collaborated subjects of business, and society. It is vital to observe how cable television is part of this expansion bring more cost with revenue, and a resource of earnings into a large market of news, and occasional entertainment. These also have become expanded news services, and information technological service providers in business that include many other subjects that requires some additional government legislative issues of consolidation. Considering this, the arbitrary interest, and cable television throughout the general public has been conditionally observant, and somewhat financially profitable. This means that during the 1990s, and the years of 2000, there have been productive years within the good, and some bad conditions of computer users with certain businesses, and company's surviving these complex new markets. Therefore even how the mass production in states like Indiana, Michigan, Ohio, and Pennsylvania are mixed with heavy industry, this includes all other states in America making some advancements to maintain these diversified markets of concerned liability for certain products, and services.

Considering most market, and business equations, including the concentration of factual markets within large products, and services most disciplines consist of lawfully important provisions. This includes the good and liable business products and employees from the top, to the bottom that is vital to manage lawfully. To manufacture large ship's, and commercial airplane's has been a vital cost managing concern. Some people in the air travel business have recognized this with the loss of various companies like TWA, PAN-AM, and others. Some of the highest cost factors within most commercial airline businesses have been pursued with labor cost, food, beverages, and alcohol, including the severe factors of maintenance and jet fuel matters. These aircrafts must have maintenance, and therefore the machinist's and mechanics pay (c/o labor unions), and work must be evaluated, and considered fairly. All these issues including the terrorist attacks on September 11, 2001 has led United Airlines Corp., and Continental Airlines Inc. (c/o market losses) to come together and form a merger to become one large company.

Within the diversified businesses, and corporations with management, and liability, some businesses have suffered with bad foreign conflicts. Continental Airlines Inc. is one of those recent companies that have endured many labor conflicts before they made a decision to merge with United Airlines Corporation. At Continental Airlines Inc. their cost issues including labor, and operating cost began to take away all their profits and liquidity applicable to profitable earnings. Upon this concern the management and the liability of the company was losing a complex battle. The "management and liability" equation has possibly benefited more foreign people, and countries then the United States, observing American citizens, and our increased conflict of taxable earnings. All relevant issue's, and officials of government in America (c/o state and federal laws) depend on tax dollars generated from the people, and the good of businesses, and corporations to operate from the cost of government. Considering some bad legislative matters that were considered with foreign people moving to America, the small business people, and owners have taken large losses within opportunities. These losses have also affected the expanded resources of American government.

The loss of business and some conditions of employment opportunities to American's considering these people who especially work, and consider investing money in a business ownership capacity are facing an economic, and social crisis. Understanding that business ownership is factually important to the individual owners, the observed rate of these people that usually try to achieve certain financial goals prior to starting a business is questionable due to government with values of some social concerns. This issue of "business startup's" have become a cautionary issue lately that has been pushed down to some of the lowest levels in American history. Some good professionals including government would observe this as an Anti-Trust law un-enforced regulated issue, and problem.

If a person, or professional observes, and compares the oil company franchise's, and some small privately owned grocery stores, some possible drug stores, and more so gas stations, certain American values where "destroyed or offset". This was established with increasingly foreign business owned conflicts, and a national security diversion during the 1990s. Most all of these businesses use to be American owned, and now a vast amount have become a monopolized controlling issue by mostly Middle Eastern people, and certain other foreign people in certain U.S. regions. American's still have the right, and concerned duty to own, invest, and operate gas stations, mini marts, and auto repair service centers, as well drug, and grocery stores. These are markets within businesses that the American society of people have worked to establish for over the last one hundred or more years. A logical factor is that these businesses don't make people rich instantly, but they are vitally important to employment, and business service operations that serve the American general public of a regional capacity. These businesses serve the American general public just as the importance of drug stores that people and doctors of internal medicine depend on for prescriptions, and professional services. Therefore this format of managing, owning, and operating the disciplines of most all American businesses is vitally responsible to the taxable conditions of citizens, and the American system of professionals, people, and government.

Considering certain businesses that don't usually consist of labor union members organizing for different causes, the diversified matter of business then must consist of stability. Between taxes, and labor unions these two issues carry important levels of awareness to be pursued with most evaluated subjects properly. These are important issues that format the American business and industrial base of conditions within stability including a good workable government that must appropriate good levels of social consolidation. These labor and non-labor equations of different businesses that are valued under the United States Constitutional laws of our American society are balanced with government intervention. This is even more so to appropriate justifiable tranquility, and prosperity within markets, people, and business.

Each, and every person, and most times their assets in America that sometimes include good labor unions have, and will continue to benefit from their part of tax dollar revenue to government that appropriates various factors of stability. It must be observed how governments tax dollar uses have offered, and provided labor unions with the lawful, and responsible right to redress government, and various amounts of corporations. These diverse issues of business/labor within good, and sometimes bad activities by labor unions is a format of working towards certain agreements, and this is observed by the hopeful prosperity of the American courts, and government. In addition the need of government, "public and private" business, and others such as non-profit organizations is an important factor for the American society to work productively together with the effort to maximize the U.S. networking of informed professionalism. Therefore the many ways that tax dollar's benefit government, business, labor unions, and the diversified markets of America is within a format of stable and prosperous conditions of liability.

The duty and liability of tax dollars appropriated throughout government in the United States including all regions, and states is a vital subject of the United States Constitutional justice within all levels of government to work together in our prosperous concern of the American society. On certain annual occasions the government from most levels of cities, towns, counties, states, and the federal jurisdictions of government have pursued the disciplines of "good and bad tax rates" to operate government for the people, and citizens.

This becomes important within protecting the American society of business, and personal assets throughout the American society of capitalized existence. Although during the late 1990s, and the early years of 2000 some Midwestern American states accumulated tax rates, and tax revenue problems which put some citizens out of their homes, and this included some businesses. This is a factual concern within how government must provide careful reviews on most tax decisions, and certain other factual duties to serve all citizens including most all small, and large business issues.

Most tax dollar, and government issues go along the facts that roads, highways, waterways, with fire, and rescue departments must be funded, and worked on as occasionally with "complicated projects made simple" to serve the American people. This includes law enforcement to provide the good within factual issues of liability to most all American local, and regional citizens, including their concept of livable standards. A sad, but perfect example is the vast amount of New Orleans citizens that broke into businesses, and stole (some needed) different product items from certain stores one day after the disaster of Hurricane Katrina. These people had recognized, and or lose faith in some conditions of our well-developed society, and government, including some valued concept of certain small, and large American business concerns. Due to this tragic factor of depression level madness within a natural disaster, the police officers of New Orleans, Louisiana where still making the effort to half-hopelessly enforce the codes of law, and order for the people, and businesses. Some of these police officer's went a-wall, and left the city, and where not to be found easily. Before the city of New Orleans completely recovers (c/o the 2005 hurricane) within residents, and businesses all of these factors will be vitally important for the respectful discipline, and process of rebuilding.

Understanding these catastrophic issues upon format within citizen asset liabilities, businesses, and government in America, various matters consisted of certain factors, and decisions. These are issues which have been appropriated with concerns of the people's important needs of when a factual emergency can, or will occur. This has also become a lazy deterrent to the effort of American small, and large businesses that could have been conducted better to help the American system of government perform better. These needs of desperate people is a factor for government to observe that before we as Americans allow foreign investors, and the many parliaments or government officials of foreign countries to earn, and control vast amounts of U.S. business investment dollars, we have issues of how the tax paying people in America should come first. In addition this includes their control of U.S. currency, and majority stock, and bond holdings in the effective nature of various American corporations.

Some of these American company's (with American Investments) sale vast amounts of products like steel, concrete, asphalt, and other ·roadway, highway, and sewer drainage components. Actually there are hundreds of thousands of products at that capacity. Even more so this applies to Americans whom have issues of employment, retirement, and secured income concerns for future years to come. This also includes everything from facilities, and roads that get older with certain up-gradable needs, and even certain conditions of child care along with healthcare matters in a family environment. These American, "social value's" along with businesses applies to American people working, and sacrificing for their Constitutional rights of American prosperity. This consideration of issues applies to a foundation of the investment dollars from certain individuals, or most valued people within American small, large, or corporate businesses.

American values, and this issue of markets are considered for labor, and businesses that are applicable to all American citizens that will work, and earn money with most levels of prosperity before they have conditional poverty issues as a problem. Then we must observe, and endure the bad decisions against others that apply to the people of the American society. The American society of business, and government has rules, and laws that include responsible duties to enforce, and comply with before the concept of social American values of liability, and most valued opportunities reach severe negative levels of disaster. In addition this is a fact of consideration of when bad foreign relations, and some American domestic professionals, or business constituents allow government, business, organized labor, and certain American markets to be ruled by foreign interest. When this happens "out of control" the good of American liberty, and certain opportunities will be factored with unconstitutional manipulation. This factual manipulation causes a lack of discipline within determination upon how our laws must prevail, and be offered prosperity. Therefore foreign and U.S. domestic business issues must be observed, and considered for any lawful issues of enforcement that applies to the American society of professionalism.

Considering British Petroleum (BP), and a few others like Bata Steel, the issue of BP, and their 2 major accidents (c/o 2005 & 2010) in 5 years, this is the problem within their disciplined control of professional (c/o some labor) values. A vast amount of oil production, steel production, and various other jobs are done by labor union members whom sometimes recognize these vital precautions. These problems of professional values consisted of negligence after accident after accident (c/o BP, Bata Steel & others) from operating a United States business or industrial process production environment, and facilities. Understanding this without the best solution of production applicable to safety, most logical details of most all technical duties becomes important, and vital. This becomes the American, and sometimes international concern of discipline with good and bad management and labor unions which both must recognize the valued issues from the top to the bottom of a company's responsibilities. These companies with issues of ownership, and management from even a worldwide (c/o BP) company, and business outlook, should have been more astute within their hazardous process facilities.

Observing certain foreign markets, and a lack of efficiency from certain American markets, and businesses observing the future possibility of existing, and present conflicts has caused a manipulated market of conditional events. The lack of hard work, and commitment by some management, and a few labor members have hurt the rich, and poor of Americans including various opportunities for people within the oil, steel, and other sectors of business. This closely looks like the same thing that has happen to the American automobile industry with the slumping sales of vehicles directly after September 11, 2001 up until the prevailing times of 2008 which doesn't seem to want to improve. Upon this understanding within business concerns most all American, and business values apply to keep operations, and markets effective.

The cost of living and the manufacturing of certain products in some other countries with different levels of inflation is a vital part of this issue within future American business conditions. If a person compares the percentage of annual profits, and earnings of some American newspaper companies, and maybe one of the American automobile companies, they can see some differences between market manipulation, and or inflation that effect's these U.S. business and certain social conditions. There are issues of business product price liability that differ from the car companies as suppose to the newspaper company that have a more complex value of liability which also reflex's the size, and cost of each of these items.

A certain amount of inflation, and more so the newspaper business issue of competition has become more active with the newly established format of "internet newspaper subscriber's". The American newspaper company's trends within sales that consist of a bit more stable, and localized market for selling their product to a logical market of people includes these regional areas that are factual. This also includes various values on their reader satisfaction rates. This concentration of most businesses with their 1ˢᵗ Amendment Rights as a low priced product with a high volume of news, and media holds the market low on manipulation, but it provides a steady format of inflation cost conditions. Observing the inflation on vehicles the price is higher, but in an economic standard within the percentage price comparison may be the same with only the style of the automobile, truck, or motorcycle products to be a consideration. Considering this, oil, gas, some steel products, and news-paper items have created good market inflation, and the awareness of foreign, and domestic competition which is part of the remaining issue within U.S. and other foreign currency rates.

The vital consideration of how the individual states, and the United States government enforces, and recognize issues of manipulation, and inflation within markets is by the executive, legislative, and judicial branches of government. This includes people that have a close concern of local businesses. Most people, and citizens that operate large, and small businesses in a region, conduct their citizenship duties in the format of working with most all government officials, and the citizens. This is the concentration of regional, and national business product, and service suppliers that must comply with lawful and reliable price matters besides controlling inflation. Observing this process within issued prices, wholesale and suggested retail prices, including cost is a formal logic of making good business decisions. The occasional concept of "price and or market" manipulation has been applied to bad issues of inflation that are usually conditional to greed, and certain criminal matters. More so business and society applies to bad issues of inflation which can be pursued by certain people whether they are in business, government, or other. This became obvious also throughout the Enron energy market business disaster.

On other occasions product improvements are another factor of what drives inflation higher within the cost of most all products, and services. Supply and demand is another one of the issues where inflation can be recognized, and then observed "hopefully" with government control. Occasionally this most times consist of the additional hard work, and the commitment of management, and or labor employee's upon which the general public, and their state of welfare will evaluate logical facts. Certain catastrophic disasters such as the hurricanes, earthquakes, floods, mudslides, terrorism, and other things that ponder an interruption to life, and businesses cause various American market activities to suffer. Some of these cost conflicts may have government subsidies to offset any extra cost (c/o damages) to a region with disaster relief conditions. This therefore can inflate the cost of operating business efficiently. All businesses must take these matters serious to keep budgets, and operating cost completely in order.

All considerations of American government have very similar duties within appropriate matters observing tax appropriated budgets, and this includes the lowest levels of unlawful manipulation possible. Mistakes can occur occasionally, but each time high rates of manipulation occur there is usually a problem of greed. When the government does not enforce this, and serve the people, and or victims including even some businesses with the best possible solutions, the people suffer a wasteful loss of tax dollar preventative concerns that add cost to other issued needs. A real but hypothetical example is that if Exxon Corporation had not been enforced to clean up their massive oil spill in the Gulf of Alaska (c/o millions & billions of dollars), the people, and animals that depend on nature to live would have been contaminated worse. This includes other lively hoods, and businesses such as fishing that would have had to spend hundreds of thousands of dollars as an industry or more to reorganize their lives, and businesses. This is valid because of the massive amount of contamination (c/o liabilities) that was applied to drinking water, and the seafood that people, and industry depend on would have been dangerously contaminated. Just as the fish and birds of the sea died, people eating these different commodities (c/o food & water) from the damaged and contaminated region would have become sick, and died also. Although a person could see the difference of this problem that occurred with warning, this was one of the highest graded issues of liability of an overall business, and governed society. Therefore this type of problem is required to appropriate all logical effort within solutions that became vital. The American people, and others where then faced with the consideration of this corporate, and regional disaster including the government that then must protect nature, and it's preservation, and wildlife for society.

Anti-Trust, Inflation, Credit, & Government Liability
(11)

CHAPTER ELEVEN
(11)

The United States Library of Congress

Anti-Trust, Inflation, Credit, & Government Liability
(11)

Within understanding, and observing the United States government, and most all individual state governments, they all consist of a format of liabilities within government regulated laws, and business matters. Considering the United States Anti-Trust (government enforcement division), and laws; these are vital government matters consisting of issues for a vast amount of businesses considering most all markets, and citizens. The citizens including most all tax paying small and large businesses depend on the United States Anti-Trust laws, and United States Constitutional laws to the format of fair, and logical business competition. These good and bad conflicts consist of lawfully fair duties, sacrifices of liability for all people, and most trusted values throughout the American general public. Then within these markets, higher levels of respected liability are proven vital for productive and fair competitive businesses in a long term effect. This format, and collaboration of issues, and subjects including the hard work of business people, and or employees is factored within the dependability of government to enforce, understand, and apply "state, and federal Anti-Trust laws".

For the many years, decades, and centuries that the American people have worked to earn money, and establish business, these are vital issues to be occasionally observed by the state, and federal courts, and the other separate branches of government. Provisional government duties such as these have been a vital part of this process, and format of business concerns for a substantial amount of years. A vast amount of the time U.S. Anti-Trust law enforcement matters can take time, and lately this has consisted of internet service and financial businesses with occasional negligence or crime. This compounded issue consisted of certain crimes that are the consideration of government solicitation for investigation, and court proceedings. The observed consideration of Anti-Trust laws, and liability (c/o SEC) legal issues are the foundation within a products lawful price that is safe, and dependable without conflict to investors, or consumers. Who invented, made, and manufactured a product is also a factor of these liabilities, and therefore U.S. Patient laws and U.S. Anti-Trust protections lawfully apply. Occasionally this includes all products, services, and certain governed business detailed issues.

The format of state government, and most all licensed professionals have a liability to the government, and citizens that is applicable to "the Constitution of the State's, and the United States federal laws". The products and services that these professionals learn about, use, and understand are factually important to residential, business, and government liabilities upon working together. During these years within the decades of the 1990s, and beyond 2008 it may become important that most state governments and the federal government consider licensing for computer programmers. This is due to the vast amount of liabilities, and the United States Anti-Trust laws that computer users, and or citizens that may, or have been affected by this technology in a negative, or unlawful capacity need. Therefore this should be considered when necessary for U.S. Constitutional Justice by the courts, and all legislature (state & federal) applicable to utility regulation & with the FCC being relevant, and vitally active for increased liability.

Considering a few professional issues, a line of occupational and professional products of regulation, and liability would be pharmaceutical products, building, and construction material products, bookkeeping and tax forms, computer programs, and other items including different types of documented books and a vast amount of tool's. An enormous amount of books are written on these subjects that include internal medicine, law, engineering, architecture, accounting, geology, sociology, computer programming, and other professional, and occupational subjects. The understanding of this applies to the occupational and professional codes of conduct including most all equipment specifications, and ethical standards, duties, and most relevant values of ethics. These important initiatives including products and professional outlined materials are recognized by government and professionals to maintain standards, and occasional "Anti-Trust disciplines" with certain values of ethics, and most considerations of factual liability.

The many issues and types of product liability concerns within the American society we live in are from time to time a result of government regulatory disciplines of enforcement. How large, and small product items in America are serviced for repair's has slightly changed for some considerations of the worse as it applies to anti-trust support issues. This, I believe is the attitude of American productivity that has taken some complex turns on small or certified repair shops, compared to the large department store chain's that repair, and service products under corporate product agreement's. All parts, and products manufactured, and sold in the United States are registered in some form with certain departments, the U.S. Patient office, and certain administrations of the U.S. government. The United States Food and Drug Administration (FDA), and the United States Department of Transportation (DOT) are two appropriate examples. Considering food, and pharmaceutical drugs are registered with the U.S. government FDA one objective is that they don't consist of any repairs like with some other products. Other products are similar to automobiles, trucks, airplanes, and locomotive trains with regulation from the DOT. Also major appliances, occasionally televisions, radios and a few other items are recognized by the U.S. Department of Energy, and regulated for content by the Federal Communication Commission (FCC) which now is also a concern for the internet broadband. Understanding the FCC with the last few Chairman's, being Michael Powell, Kevin Martian, and now Julius Genachowski have consisted of working disciplines that are tremendously important. These regulated disciplines consist of small and large systems such as the good, and bad of arbitrary internet computer systems including cell phones, television, radio, and commercial satellites to be part of state, and federal regulatory enforcement. This means that the products and most all parts are registered annually, and are recognized with government as a factor of various disciplines of certain product requirements, and their format of secured liability.

Considering the format, and resource of the people with more liability from the government's responsibility to recognize the lawful differences between department stores, and certain corporate products, certain U.S. Anti-Trust laws, and patient rights are an occasional concern. This includes the different parts of industry that come real close together with similar products. These concerns are diversified within business, and therefore these subjects have various market concerns. Observing, and understanding that this also consist of the sales of products, and then the potential service of them including how most products are registered with the state, and or federal government, some of the only issues that occasionally apply is how they were made within manufacturing. A few good corporate examples are the former Montgomery Ward's Corp, the Sears Corp, J.C. Penney's Corp, the Ford Motor Company, General Electric Corp, and the Raytheon Company. This diversified group of businesses consist of a vast amount of product components that include sales, services, and manufacturing with applicable liability (c/o Anti-Trust laws or agreements) to various factors that are applicable to government standards in America. High rates of liability is most all the time established for the customers that "purchases, and depend" on these corporate products from various establishments of manufacturing at various retail store businesses.

From my experience, and understanding of sales, and repair's at major department stores this was a very important liability within the purchase of a product, and its long term use by the customer. This is a consistent business priority within the wholesale, and retail sales process of agreements. Some of the valued business concerns that the Montgomery Ward's department stores would provide is repair's to most all major appliance's that they sale. This factual concept of business includes all name brands that were sold at Montgomery Ward's stores. These stores during the 1970s, and 1980s had service repair shops at a large number of store locations that included some service repairs at a customer's home. This almost was a competitive issue against the Sears (Maytag) repair people, and their service commitment. Considering this, Montgomery Ward's Corporation had its own name brand of major appliance's including lawn equipment, but also they would sale other corporate name brands, such as General Electric, Westinghouse, AT&T, Toro, and others. Montgomery Ward's Corp, and a few other major department stores would also use major corporate manufactures as contractors to create their own name brand products similar to items like entertainment systems, and lawn equipment. Their next format of business is that they would service all name brand appliances that they sold, and this would consist of customer satisfaction agreements, and warrantees. This was a product, and service practice that was matched within most major department stores including Sears & Robuck, and certain J.C. Penney's Department Store Corporation locations. A competitive lead on these business subjects was held by part of their "Winning Ways" of business solutions.

These were productive years for these types of department store corporations, and even their commitment of liability to their customers. Upon comparing the years of the 1970s, 80s, the 90s, and "now", this service process has weaken. The high levels of good liability can still be found, but some customer satisfactory purchases has diminished with certain levels of economic, or service business decision making. An economic example of the changing times is that within the purchase of one, two or a logical number of home telephones where purchased within the years before the 1990s, and now some people may buy 4 or 5 wireless telephones in a year by year process. Ironically the big customer satisfaction, and wireless telephone product competitors are Apple Computer Corp, Comcast Corp, LG Electronics, and a few others with AT&T still making conditional presence, but most all have purchase plans that occasionally effect the credit markets.

During the 1960s, and 1970s a telephone in the home would be purchased or provided by the phone company (AT&T and Western Electric) as a format of customer considerations, and this appropriated the satisfactory use of a lower maximum amount of telephones for years. Considerably these wireless telephones with other devices that are internet accessible with other features like camera's, are also much more expensive. Therefore how we adapt to the cost of new technology is also part of our values within personal management.

As certain payment processes has changed, the concept of lay-a-way programs in most retail stores have been almost slightly removed or eliminated. A formal resource of credit card's has taken the place of most lay-a-way purchases, and this is a different purchase process for the customers. This is the format of where cost factors, and product purchase considerations have affected the American economic concept of normal life, and even some businesses. The largest concentration of U.S. Anti-Trust laws have not effected department stores so much as it was found necessary in the "American Telephone industry", and more so the "American Oil industry"

With vast amounts of credit card plans, and lending available today this has applied additional cost, and rationing of commend sense evaluations that may not be so common to all people. This new credit card out-burst of issues within the American changing times has helped department stores cut back, or eliminate access inventory, and backed up repair orders at various store locations. Then the cost is advanced with interest to the purchasing consumer's within the people, and the inventory which sometimes moves faster with the credit card company seeming to earn a profit. The customer can spend more money, and advance or exceed their credit limits, and this has factored a new concern that personal spending means people must have discipline. Consumer spending at this capacity also may require help for the American system of government. Considerably this is valued on occasions to help the people recover or observe conflicting lending rates upon enforcing that credit card interest rates maintain controlled stability. Even the large consumer electronic manufactures such as General Electric, and Westinghouse occasionally have a format within their credit liability spending. What this simply means is that everyone must observe bookkeeping, or the managing of money just like a check book, or credit card account compared to people or most business income. Therefore these new factors of credit exist from the smallest of money managing, to the largest of keeping finances, and credit in complete order including rates of interest.

One important and appropriate reason why the United States government has a U.S. Anti-Trust law duty, and obligation to help the people is due to the factor of complicated, or fraudulent debt that can occur. Another concern is that large corporate funded businesses are not the easiest group of people with total fairness to compete against in business, or the court; observing individuals, and small businesses. This is the consideration that large department stores, and corporations can go out of business with innocent people owning them money (c/o harassment from bill collectors) if harmful business decisions are logically observed throughout these corporations. A factual problem considering this is observed when people understand the need, or reason for buying certain products, but the company providing these products occasionally may have managing disciplinary problems. The good and bad of managing problems should have been considered lawfully better ether in business or in the courts if considered appropriately. This also applies a better rate of business survival with productive outcomes of income earnings, and product disciplinary factors.

Just as the United States government during 2007 has released studies that imply issues about our American consumer spending, and certain business economic issues, various credit problems, and inflation is out of control, or under close observation. This is the fact of various people that have exceeded normal spending, and negligence with inflation which has increased other service banking matters with inflated fees on regular procedures like document request on occasions. These are the results of bad business or even government decisions, such as with uneducated mortgage lenders that where discovered in California, and a few other states. Other issues of inflation are the cost of products, and or service issues within the American society, and markets that cannot be avoided when productive duties are applied lawfully. Within this formatted concern of cash, and credit, the cost of food, gas, and other items of importance have reached unreal levels of normal purchasing capacity. During 2010 the state of California government budget crisis, and matters have gotten so bad that food stamp programs increased, and various conditions of certain welfare programs (c/o other state government's) are partly being eliminated. Therefore the 2009, and 2010 economic crisis is effecting government, and businesses more, and more. This has factored some businesses to be operated in a negative balance sheet of responsible operating procedures, and this effects most all people involved.

Vast amounts of households including government taxable resources are also being affected at historical rates. When these business factors are pursued out of a controlled balance of budget spending, or disciplines, this is when good businesses make an effort to reorganize with efficiency in a productive and lawful capacity. To correct these problems American businesses sometimes cannot accomplish certain goals, or operating standards by themselves. It also consisted of a level of required good government decisions with commitments. This commitment of government duties, and business working together on economics, infrastructures, and other involved business issues has relevance just as we observe hurricane Katrina, and other disasters that hurt local businesses when government missed an important issue. This becomes a vital equation for American economics within the financial balance sheets of planning and controlled budgets lawfully, and that includes with productive responsibilities. These are disciplined resources throughout our governed U.S. society, and most all businesses that must be observant for future prosperity.

The United States government, and certain corporations such as General Electric, Raytheon, and AT&T have worked together (c/o logical business distance) for years in certain different ways. Besides the consideration of these businesses being contractors, and vendors to government including even the U.S. Department of Defense, and others, these contractors have the American Society of Tested Materials in common. These are factors within product material specifications of American standards that consist of buy-product materials that have various standards that enter-phase on similar established products. These by-product standards have quality and manufactured importance to GDP rates upon which consist of how they occasionally have important financial exchange values. This becomes important within most common, and vital data on economics, and more so product liability standards within the responsible manufacturing of product part's that from time to time consist of ware & tear maintenance.

The General Electric Corporation sale's the United States government National Atmospheric Space Administration (NASA) components for their resource of solar energy collectors for electricity in orbit. Also they sale the United States government National Oceanic Atmospheric Administration (NOAA) meteorology equipment, and lighting systems upon which also includes even government electrical power distribution equipment. The Raytheon Company sales the United States government large missile systems considering they also manufacture small jet aircrafts. The American Telephone & Telegraph Corporation sales the United States government equipment for their telephone, and communication needs with responsible service connections. Considering these, and so many other United States government contractors, this is done on a level of responsible liability within most formal conditions of ethics, and workable standards. Therefore this market and process becomes aggressive, but lawful within these formal issues of business with the United States federal government.

Doing business in the market of government contractors consisting of sales is a broad, but disciplined process of diversified products, and services. Most of these large contactors understand the format of ethics that is pursued within most of these good, and bad ways to consolidate perfection in the markets of government contracting. Within the format of productive business concerns, most United States government contractors are very much so occasionally at near public monopoly status within products, or services for the government. Some of these companies are more so considered as a conglomerate instead of a public utility (c/o public monopoly) because of their complex business operations that may include some confidential biding to serve particular regions. These are facts on what certain products and services the government needs, and depend on with agreements, and most time U.S. Anti-Trust requirements. An appropriate example is within the U.S. Anti-Trust laws applicable to the resource of business conditions of John D Rockefeller (c/o Standard Oil) in the "Oil Industry", and Alexander G Bell (c/o AT&T) in the "Telephone Industry" from the early 1900s to the years of 1990, and 2000. These businesses and people with inventions, products, services, and sales throughout the United States made powerful earnings. The value of these resources had vigorous legal arguments, and established numerous company's in various parts of America with certain business product, and service advancements with multiple, but limited name changes.

Considering mass production and corporate responsibilities, these public, private businesses are occasionally considered as public monopolies that consist of high grades of liability within their disciplines of business, and professionalism. This complies with how corporation's and firms do business with each other, the American general public, and the American system of government. Their format, and logic to provide a product, or service for the American general public that is most times paid for by the U.S. government to certain corporations is then a commitment between them both, and the American citizens. Observing the thousands of diversified small, or large businesses for any form of government in America, the compliance of "state and federal Constitutional Laws" are a vital part of these diverse markets. Understanding this relevant factor the government usually pays a good and logical price for the products, and services that they consider to buy. This outlines disciplines within the government for the quality, and efficiency concerning the concept of high professional standards.

Quality and high standards within these markets of government contracts consist of tax payer input, most tax dollar purchase output disciplines, and other factors of confidential, and business confirmed transactions. The large factor of American businesses that the states, and U.S. federal government recognizes, and dose consider "concerning business" is a format within most all the time to make the best effort to keep taxable, and government liability issues completely productive, and in order. Within the largest corporations in American business, this is a day by day concern as well within what corporations will appropriate concerning financial disciplines on a quarterly base of earnings most all the time. Each quarter of earnings annually that consist of losses or gains at a professional firm, or corporation within disclosed earnings is a productive evaluation of progressive awareness. Therefore even some small businesses that consist of negative and positive earnings with tax matters are calculated as tax values, and government appreciation including all investment prosperity factors.

Within how we as American business constituents estimate all the financial and economic conditions of business this is a disciplinary part, and or vital subject within the American money circulation. Some of these money circulation concerns consist of the taxable processes of lawful government appropriations which are considered relevant issues. When all public, private or government contracts within earnings are involved, this gives the corporation or business an idea of speculation on how their economic annual outlook will end up. This is the money circulation that also helps the U.S. Currency rate maintain stable product, and service values of appropriate discipline, and prosperity. During the years of the early 2000s, and now 2007 these estimated earnings (c/o the U.S. Currency) have provided some good towards foreign constituents to establish income, and leaving a vast amount of Americans without investment dividends, and being victimized by credit interest rate increases.

The factor of investment dividends in the American economy upon losing investment dollars to foreign countries, and foreign investors is a big factual loss to the well-developed American society of today, and the future. From 2005 to 2010 there has been, hundreds of corporations, and publicly held companies that have suspended their stock dividend payments. A few big examples are Ford Motor Company, General Motors Corporation, Chrysler Corporation, an enormous amount's of banks, and even businesses like AIG Inc, and the State Farm Insurance Company which have seen other severe business change's. Concerning this problem a severe level of American investors (c/o some international issues) is within the amount of needed support for American business, and employment opportunities for these money circulating issues. This money making process is valid within stock shareholder dividends, and earned income investment dollars to be a part of productive growth mostly in America as it may apply to other countries. This is known American Capitalism, and applicable to Market Capitalism for liabilities within capital gains, and valid liquidity. The local, state, and federal government with various constituents then can appropriately offer regional contractors, and citizen's vast amounts of income and employment earning opportunities. These opportunities consist of the occupational and professional resources to upgrade certain government infrastructures with a balanced budget. Upon these tax dollar investments for small or large businesses, or corporations with employment this improves the many conditions of their capital markets, and business quality factors with strong liquidity.

American investment dollars from citizens are vitally important from individuals, and or corporations including the small, large, public, private businesses that offer financial gains, and investment returns. In addition this helps most cities and towns with municipal bonds, and where they have an established format of business operation's doing good in the right direction. The American investments that are supported by the liability of government, and the U.S. Anti-Trust laws helps this process, and smaller productive businesses expand with personal, and business prosperity. American taxable business earnings that consist of losses, and more so gains was observed productively after the Pearl Harbor attacks, and then the American economy was disciplined for American values, employment, investments, and business earnings for all productive citizens. This format, and period of American business progress was maintained up until almost the end of the Vietnam War during the early 1970s. This therefore is vital to understand, and observe the economic gains, and losses of American businesses, and the tax base including investments. Considering this format, it is too great to ignore, and allow the wrong unlawful foreign interference to the values of American businesses. Therefore government must be outlined with logical agendas, including its most applied resources of tax paying businesses in a workable, and logical governed capacity. This is more so relevant from government decisions by the Securities and Exchange Commission, and others that must enforce laws, and keep U.S. investors, and businesses productive.

Business losses and gains by way of investments in public companies just like losses, or gains in private companies have occurred for years, and this always requires corrections. The public held company will usually answer to more investors on these subjects. Within correcting problems in business, and more so government this does not require war all the time, or trying to change all the social problems of America, but aggressive decisions with less conflicts, or crime is or may be necessary. The September 11, 2001terrorist attacks where a large part of business losses, and now have provided a war time contributory factor of government losses from various conditions in the American society. Valuable corrections consist of hard work, and good decision making within various business, and government details, but people cannot always be replaced easily. To most productive business owners and employees a correction means improving products, services, and other manageable duties including issues of the daily business operation. Then to recognize when possible losses will exceed the cost of operating the business, this is always a vital speculation that protects the investments, investors, and business.

The United States Securities and Exchange Commission (SEC) has provided some good and bad resources of enforcing the laws concerning investments, and business. Contrary to this enforcement concern the most vital facts of enforcing SEC regulation are the managing concept of individuals, and complaints. These complaints most times have been factored with duties to provide the best effort including the awareness of government issues. Both the state, and federal format of American government has laws (c/o the U.S. SEC) that requires business to disclose information to investors, and some investors, and businesses to the Securities and Exchange Commission upon working with various businesses, and society. This discipline with SEC disclosure laws is of an anti-trust value that controls the conditionally very rich investors from illegally controlling the sacrifices of the expanding small investors with growing businesses in a public traded company or the consideration of this public offering process without illegal disruption. Making, or achieving informative past, and present appropriate business plans with productive activities is a lawful outline within these issues of profitable gains, and losses that are, and can be economically controlled.

The liability of individual, corporate, or small business complaints to the Securities and Exchange Commission can correct unlawful or bad decisions (c/o some U.S. SEC decisions) that effect business, and investments. In the financial brokerage industry of business concerns, small and large businesses operating at high rates of capacity are providing liquidity to investment banks. These investment banks would not have hardly anything without these product, and service disciplines of American business, and capitalism that must keep adequate bank disciplines of efficiency. During 2008 and 2009 the investment bank criminal act of Bernard Madoff was criminally acknowledged by government prosecutors going back to the mid-1990s within accumulating billions of investment banking dollar assets. Bernard Madoff did this without honoring the most important, and lawful duty of investing his clients liquidity of cash assets honestly. These cash assets belonging to other people where illegally abused by not pursuing those investment dollars (c/o a Ponzi Scheme) to the requested corporate or financial investments from those investor-clients.

Financial losses accumulated for thousands of people, businesses, and organizations with Bernard Madoff, and some others as financial professionals involved in the concept of financial losses with negligence, and more so the intent to commit financial crime's. The Bernard Madoff scandal, and other scandals have taking away, or distorted some of the most important conditions of liability that exist between banking, and investment banking that consist of their agreements with individual investors, and businesses. Large, and small investment banks, and corporate management officials have engaged in scandals that financially harm other businesses, and this makes them wealthy before being caught, and prosecuted. The level of financial crimes can also be part of U.S. Anti-Trust law violations when manipulated harm to small productive businesses consist of discretionary conflicts. All investment bankers, and corporate management officials that achieve good levels of wealth are not involved in certain financial conditions of crime, but they pursued things with a value of good, bad, or risky sacrifices of commitments. United States Anti-Trust laws can be abused when a small investment bank company obtains critical information about smaller businesses that put them out of business. Then within their wrongful act the other business is prosecuted for something such as fraud which means more than 2 businesses suffer. These conflicts are "sometimes" caused by people that solicit growing, and or prosperous business owners, or businesses, and people. This is the format of when long-term and short-term decisions are set as goals, and their sacrifices are not achieved with various minor conflicts (c/o trust-busting) that cause deterred business, and or even conflicting social factors.

A relevant concern to the economic conditions of 2007 have accumulated losses that would put the United States in a near recession, and approaching a depression with corporate financial losses. These losses have occurred in the banking industry with companies like Washington Mutual losing over $900 million dollars in their 2007 annual report. The Merrill Lynch Investment Bank Company reported losses of over $8 billion dollars in 2007. There has been three small airline companies that have filed for bankruptcy protection, and this conflict within process procedures occurred nearly leaving American people stranded in far-away locations. Within these horrifying business factors a vast amount of solutions within business, and government reorganizing will be needed even though this is the normal, but occasional conflicting process of business.

The solution's for a bad economy is one thing for business, but the effect for the individual American citizens is a vital array of issues to be addressed. Between the years of 1975, and 1978 the city of Gary, In., and Northwest Indiana suffered a depressed economic cycle that affected a vast amount of young workers in the steel industry. These types of hard times within economic conditions causes people's plans of retirement, future healthcare, and other things of concern to considerably suffer with difficulties. Certain considerations of effort are looked at within the capacity of what government can do to eliminate some of these financial burdens. Within how all people in society, business, and government have a discipline of working together when they must be logical to find solutions, these various problems are a value of American ethical standards. These become the formal considerations of these transitional times that will be reconsolidated for most good, and bad decisions of leadership that are valued with the understandable hope that most all improvements will be a factor within future stability.

The Effect Of Corporate Mergers And Buyouts
In America
(12)

CHAPTER TWELVE
(12)

The United States Library of Congress

The Effect Of Corporate Mergers And Buyouts
In America
(12)

Considering the diversified business markets of America, a variation of small, and large businesses upon vitally including corporation's in the United States have been subjected to a variation of corporate merger's, and buyout's. These corporate merger's, and buyout's whether hostile or agreed as non-hostile mergers or buyout acquisitions have consisted of many different societal effects. Upon this concept of business procedures it's similar to one citizen buying a small business from another citizen with appropriate agreements. This effect on the American society is occasionally tremendous as it applies to the people as employees, the business owners within making the best decisions possible, and even the American system of government.

During the late 1980s the American financial markets went thru a vast amount of financial transactions that where considered as acquisitions within mostly corporate buyouts, and occasional corporate mergers. Some of the corporation's that where involved with effects to the Corporate American society where RJ Reynolds Tobacco Company, Eastman Kodak Corporation, Sterling Drug Corporation, Motown Records Inc., MCA Incorporated (*Music City Corporation of America), Pullman Company, and various others. Years later during the 1990s, a junk bond market seem to be slightly out of control within some banking, and corporate buyouts included the mergers of Chemical Bank (Corp), Manufactures Hanover Bank (Corp), and even the activity at Chase Manhattan

Banking Company becoming JP Morgan Chase Banking Corporation. Within these banks, and corporations including some steel manufacturing companies these where a few transactions that seem to be companies that purchased businesses, merged, or where bought-out with the effort of restructuring the business operation. This was the concern most times to construct the management into being a more effective corporation within productive business issues that occasionally included good, and bad foreign relations. Considering this a certain large capacity of capital gains within assets where acquired, and this created financial wealth for some, but not completely all as an entire business operation of success.

These merger factors may have worked fairly "good" within some like the Exxon Corporation, and the Mobil Oil Corporation becoming ExxonMobil Corporation. Then the corporate buyout conducted by British Petroleum Company buying Amoco Oil Corporation of America was slightly different including certain foreign relation "concerns", and a major accident not long after completion of the acquisition. Also during these years of the 1990s the Digital Equipment Corporation seemed to be a business that became severely isolated with the potential of needing a good or proper type of merger, or buyout. A more relevant conflict within a foreign business group of people from South Korea (c/o LG) bought a controlling stake, and majority interest of stock in the Zenith Corporation. Besides manufacturing television's the Zenith Corporation from time to time in different American war's was an important United States Department of Defense contractor providing radar, and communication equipment. Therefore considering the Korean War with the heavy involvement of the United States during the 1950s this merger / buyout "during the 1990s" consisted of some national security concerns with American valued technology. Then foreign and U.S. domestic issued conflicts occurred throughout the multiple acquisition's within the business mergers of certain telephone companies, and the big loser's within WorldCom Corporation, and Enron Corporation. Therefore this explains why the global community and concept of business is quite different even with the loss of American businesses, especially as it applies to American issues of professionalism, and some concerned values of the U.S. Constitution.

These diversified corporations during the years of 1986 to 1998 had enormous amounts of money, and asset transactions, but not with all businesses completely providing an increase in Gross Domestic Product rates, and sales. Although some businesses have done well concerning these factors that include productive services when businesses deem liable, it is vital that these American businesses maintain even better productive rates of business. A large rate of individuals (c/o billionaires) became very wealthy, and leading up to the years of 2005 to 2008 vast amounts of American employees of certain businesses where subjected to becoming unemployed. This problem and issue of people becoming wealthy, and others becoming poor was caused by some of these same various individuals (c/o business) within destructive conflicting business, and corporate operations. Some would say derivatives, and hedge funds were part of the misguided financial market, and economic crisis of conflict. In addition to product sales, and services considering the year of 2009 some of the highest rates of unemployment filing clams in American history has hit the American society with decisive economic and financial conflicts. Understanding this, various American businesses did not expand, but certain individual American businesspeople, and their financial wealth did expand extensively. Therefore during the 1st decade of 2000 some logical effects form the American society of business has not offered overall prosperity, just like some corporate buyouts have strange repercussions.

A vast amount of American public and private businesses (c/o employment & production) has outlined that most levels of government must do more to help the American merger / buyout equation business process improve. The subsidiary businesses apart from regional or metropolitan rates of employment within these corporations are usually the first to be hit with budget cuts where certain jobs are eliminated to observe future productive business concerns. This is closely relevant within the automobile industry with the troubles at the Ford Motor Company, General Motors Corporation, and Chrysler Corporation upon which (a percentage of Chrysler in 2008) was bought-out by Cerberus Capital Management which now holds a majority amount of stock in the Chrysler Corporation. After this large business merger transaction of stocks purchased, certain Chrysler Corp models, and plants where cut financially form production, but bankruptcy conflicts where becoming their other real challenge.

Considering the year of 2009 the Chrysler Corporation, and General Motors Corporation began discussing possible bankruptcy proceedings that could be very complex for the American society of workers, other businesses, and a vast amount of consumers. Throughout the next few months both company's (GM & Chrysler) filed bankruptcy with General Motors coming out of bankruptcy in less than 2 months. Observing 2010 both company's still consist of severe financial problems while even numerous American airline companies are making arrangements to merge. As this circulation of financial effects makes ration to an economic slow-down, various amounts of American citizens are affected. Considering this, American citizens, and certain employees in the auto industry have suffered similar to others industries. The suffering also includes their stalled or isolated habits of work that have been reduced or critically affected as in a recession becoming close to a depression with various big companies agreeing to "corporate mergers" to survive in this American business environment. This is similar to the self-service pick up window for quick and hopefully productive results like satisfying hunger, only it's an economic issue of terror or turmoil that keeps getting worse. Corporate America, and some government concerns may have let this level of "Unconstitutional greed", and lack of business prosperity during the early 1990s bring our level of Constitutional business tranquility to an all-time low.

To understand a more formal concept within the corporate America merger or buyout process, a businessperson or a corporate board must evaluate the valued cost, or estimated value of a company. Then the purchasing company has to determine how much it will need to run the company in a better direction. Even in the hostile corporate takeover buyout process a corporate buyout raider would acquire over time a controlling amount of the stock in a corporation, but the U.S. Securities and Exchange Commission and the U.S. Congress created a 10% stock purchase discloser rule within laws. This format of a regulated rule on anonymously acquiring large sums of a corporation's stock is vital to the stability of a productive corporate management's concerns of lawful liability. The stock and bond prices (c/o assets and liabilities) usually appropriate the value of the business, and all outstanding shares of available stock at common, and preferred price values. Usually this junk bond process of purchasing a company can be beneficial to the resource of a similar or competing company upon which one is ready to go out of business, and negotiations can be established between the two known business corporate owners. This is the financial equation of vast amounts of people or board members, and employees on both corporate sides, and most small or large institutional investors. Although it's not all the time that employees of the purchasing company may see additional money real soon, but a financial effect is usually relevant within time. In fact, these transactions have certain levels of risk that require the concentration of management to work a bit harder keeping all productive resources in workable productive order.

The RJ Reynolds Tobacco Company over a vast amount of years earlier purchased numerous smaller companies that consist of food products that are items bought in most grocery stores. Then during 1987 the company was the target of a corporate takeover buyout by Kohlberg, Kravis, Roberts & Company (KKR) investment banking. During this stock purchase transaction the RJ Reynolds stock price went from $55.00 a share to around the tender offer accepted price of $109.00 a share. During this process and transaction the RJ Reynolds Co. stock price topped out at over $120.00 a share. This process went on for over five (5) and a half (½) weeks making the stock active with the two (2) companies negotiating a tender offer for all stock's and bond's. Therefore this gave the KKR Investment Company an issued condition of future control, and concern within a group of different top management officials.

The buyout anticipation within planning of what would happen to the RJ Reynolds Tobacco Company and its assets is that the KKR investment banking operation was planning to sale certain RJ Reynolds subsidiary businesses for profit. Considering this level of business anticipation the business plan of Kohlberg, Kravis, Roberts, and Company was to hold the company private, and pursue increased or steady earnings with the company, and subsidiaries doing good business. The present RJ Reynolds tobacco business operation was not affected, but it was reorganized slightly as a private company, including its subsidiaries which consisted of Winston, Camel, and Salem cigarettes. Other subsidiaries of RJ Reynolds Tobacco Company are the enormous business operations of RJR Nabisco with Shredded Wheat, Oreo cookies, Ritz crackers, Planters peanuts, Life Savers, and Del-Monte fruits and vegetables, that where somewhat reorganized, and considered for sale. Throughout a vast amount of years and decades these corporate brands, including products earn productive amounts of revenue, and this declared them excellent products to the American society.

The concept within profit taking, and sales of most corporate subsidiary businesses is occasionally viewed for management to create the same or more so a better business level of progress. Although when the original business operation and owners has changed, this progress is important considering that the right type of hard work goes in with the right levels of productive business decisions. Considering this the company is split up into different pieces with complex changes of more so the process of restructuring the entire business. This process was considered to become the same if it was just for the leveraged money, or to be a more productive corporation applicable to the U.S. Constitution, and laws within the most productive resources of business possible. Understanding this, the formal factor of why some large businesses with growth remain private companies includes their distinct caution to avoid instability about being a public traded company. Establishing these companies and businesses are a consideration of value on any stock exchange until all valued, and certain massive resources apply. Contrary to this caution it has consistently been a working process for the good of business financial underwriters, and the conclusive values like at the Microsoft Corp., Apple Computer Corp., and a vast amount of others like some productive food processing businesses or corporations. Therefore these are not close to being junk bond takeover issues of consideration, but they are valued businesses that various people take serious.

During 1988 the Sterling Drug Company was bought-out by the Eastman Kodak Company of Rochester, New York. Observing the concerned issues of the Sterling Drug Company, the Eastman Kodak Company reviewed this company as a business operation with troubled assets, and certain other useful pharmaceutical and chemical products including manufacturing processing. These are part of the marketable business divisions, chemical products, and levels of production that the Eastman Kodak Company could utilize, sale, or enhance within certain productive ways that already exist in their normal and massive business process. The Eastman Kodak Company mastered this production format within processes over time which has been part of their camera film, camera parts, and chemical product manufacturing business in the United States sense the late 1880s with the founder George Eastman. Within the consideration of Eastman Kodak it has enhanced their chemical business operation within an additional unit as the "Eastman Chemicals" Co. and therefore the prosperous buyout of Sterling Drugs over the years has made a productive return which is helpful to the company, and some concerns of the American society.

Considering the economic crisis of 2009 the Eastman Kodak Corporation has suffered some ups, and downs financially like other businesses, and citizens. Contrary to this fact they have maintained a level of stable business, and earnings with minor layoffs. Then the corporation had similarities of conflict to some other large businesses like at General Electric Corporation, and more so Exxon (c/o ExxonMobil) Corporation. These issues of a problem with new decision's, and conflicts within management, and corporate employee procedures, this is the obligation of controlling a larger corporation that will consist of a few conditions of the changing times. Therefore this became the purchased agreement buyout, and or merger "after effect" of another company with good, and bad issues which have additional resources to consider. These resources over the years have involved certain complicated issues within a productive and workable capacity, but they are still constantly reviewed.

The merger, and buyout activity at General Electric Corporation has been conducted with vast amounts of business inputs, and outputs to sale unproductive business subsidiaries of the GE holding company business plan. This corporate buyout activity issue put the leadership of Jack Welch, and GE in the upper part of the list of "corporate raiders" as being a CEO that implies that the company must perform or we will sale! This was similar to the game monopoly, which consist of good, and bad concerns within business decisions, and the luck within (c/o rolling dice) of understanding the diversified times of society. Within the consideration of the General Electric Corporation, and other similar corporations when the concept of a junk bond market has left them with businesses (c/o small corporations) that they cannot use, or make productive, there is an effort to sale this failing or unvalued business unit. The National Broadcasting Company (NBC) has been a fairly productive subsidiary of General Electric Corporation sense the 1980s. Before that, NBC was a large subsidiary of the RCA Corporation (formerly *Radio Corporation of America) which has various conditions of diversified business resources.

One consideration of this factual problem concerning the quality of business issue's, is that the General Electric Corporation is not alone in the consideration of unaffordable, unprofitable, or unwanted businesses. During 2008 there are banks, brokerage firms, and even department stores like Circuit City Electronics Co. that investors or financial institutions don't want with their troubled businesses combined throughout the American economy. Motown Records Corporation "formerly" and founded in Detroit, Michigan by Berry Gordy upon which their business slightly suffered a slowdown, consisted of certain economic troubles. Motown Records Corp as a private company was productive during the 1960's, and 70's with prosperous value, but in the late 1980s the business was congested with slow sales, and conflicting issues within the management of earnings. These are some of the problems that made the business become slightly isolated with film productions, and certain personal conflicts that did not help gross earning's heavily.

Contrary to the business years, and time of isolation at Motown Records Corporation this was a company of respected integrity, upon which included it's many successes of black entertainment holdings, and then they were bought-out by MCA Incorporated. Actually between Diana Ross, Somkey Robinson, Steve Wonder, and the Temptations (c/o other constituents) which are the artist whom always stayed committed, or slightly returned to Motown Records, there is a perceptional value considering Steve Wonder is the only one who is still committed to the Motown label. In a more logical reference it seems that almost every known to date music academy in American has provided music awards to the professional career of Steve Wonder, and that slightly explains some parts and the history of the "Record Label of Motown" Corporation. Observing this, sometimes the American system of financial markets has good and bad days including years like during 1929, the mid 1970s, and other periods of economic concern where regions and conditional businesses suffer. This economic cycle implies with meaning that the times may be tuff in various economic or financial ways observing regional markets, but people, and businesses within American markets must achieve lawful survival.

Some of the most complex corporate mergers where with the Manufacture Hanover Bank, and the Chemical Bank (c/o New York City) that had a combined merger value of over $135.0 billion dollars during the turn of the 1990 decade. Now considering the years of 2000 neither of these two banks, are traded individually on any stock exchange in the United States. Considering they do have a relevant business, at this time they do not consist of any major business activity except bank holding, and extensive property management disciplines. This is quite different from the business activities they consisted of in the late 1970s, and early to mid-1980s. The merger of Manufacture Hanover Bank, and Chemical Bank seemed to be negotiated right down the middle. This became the future extent of these two (2) bank businesses which included both CEO's John Gillicuddy of Manufactures Hanover Bank serving first as CEO for a concept of yearly terms. Then another negotiated term consisted of Walter Shipley of Chemical Bank taking the other scheduled CEO term for a conditional number of years of this newly merged banking business operation. This merger consisted of the loss of more than 6000 employees from conditionally some bad lending issues as (2) separate banking businesses with certain up's, and down's throughout regional business concerns. Both of these banks now consist of a single local commerce banking operation with business activity mostly under the Chemical Bank business name with Manufacturers Hanover Trust company resources.

The observation between the many people that suffered from the junk bond madness of both Enron Corporation, and WorldCom Corporation was good with raising short-term capital, but terrible with long-term economic values of liquidity, and productive or responsible business security. These two corporate businesses consisted of a lack of productive management, and liquidity. This included the destructive values especially with Enron Corporation working to manage an oversized market within the public utilities of electrical energy in certain regions of America. Now the American society is still adjusting to the liquidation of these corporate conflicts after nearly 20 years of these businesses buying other businesses which had certain U.S. Anti-Trust law violation concerns. This was done many times to become some of the biggest business operations, but some would say they were like a complex set of corporate bully's. Upon this, the "biggest corporation in the world scenario", distinctively doesn't always mean the business was built to the most productive, and efficient corporation. Upon this observation the vital operating condition of the size, and valued business production of discipline is substantially not always managed for the most productive, and or profitable results.

Within the consideration to expand a business operation thru mergers, and corporate business buyout conditions this is occasionally a lazy factor that accumulated severe losses within long-term financial matters. Contrary to the indifference, a buyout can help a logical expansion, "if" it's done at a responsible capacity for the truly good of most business decisions. This seems to work properly for one (1) out of every fifty (50) businesses that try it, and therefore it's not a good business technique, and plan, unless complete "applicable effort is applied". Most normal business plans in America do consist of money issues, but the format within factors of progress consist of the best managing of products, and or services including cost that the new or productive business offers. These values within the managing of all conditions of asset liquidity, and even subjects like manufacturing consist of values that are also important to a prosperous future. This therefore becomes the effort of American business resources that the American people appreciate, and occasionally this is passed on to the employee's, and business owners.

Considering some acquisitions of corporate merger's, and buyouts the effect is occasionally observed different within a vast amount of products, and services by businesses where various issues of employment and governed tax revenue is affected. All levels of government recognize the loss of certain businesses, but more so the local cities, and towns are hit the hardest as it concerns their economic resources of a regional money circulation that is reduced or eliminated. Between 1995, to 2005 more cities and town's observe department stores like Montgomery Wards, Service Merchandise, Zayre, and others go out of business. Then during that time Enron Corporation, and WorldCom Corporation provided additional failure, and harm to government, and the people upon which these corporations made some corporate mergers/buyouts seem worse than bankrupt businesses or failing companies. These problems also effected other small and large corporations close to these businesses, with a conditional amount of innocent investors, and a vast amount of similar conflicts which caused other economic hardships for years to come.

Years after the loss of this vast amount of corporate department store businesses, and other businesses, a concentrated factor of American governed economic, and vital tax revenue was eliminated. These tax revenue factors consisted of the people working for these department stores which had an understanding of this loss of corporate American values and stability. This is part of what citizens, and local government missed within the tax paying generated dollars that these businesses appropriated for the American society during decades, and years of prosperity. In addition a massive loss of jobs, and businesses filing for bankruptcy following these economic tuff times have been a severe strain. Although Wal-Mart Corp, and a few others made some parts of a tax revenue replacement possible, these resources were not completely enough. Then this serious effect was partly causing problems to the extent of issues of an economic, employment, and social slow down which became tremendous. In addition a slow-down in most all corporate buyouts seemed to follow as no other businesses could compensate these overall losses. This business purchase process has been limited to some totally isolated companies except for certain emergency relief issues of corporate or business purchase buyouts.

During 2009 the rate of unemployment has reached some of the highest levels in the history that the United States has ever kept on record. This rate of unemployment can be compared to certain industry conflicts during the 1970s following the "Vietnam War", which was followed by a decade later with an American junk bond market that increased activity that became (c/o laws and business) out of control. Even the amount of financial brokers (c/o the 1980s) violating the insider trading SEC rules, and laws to earn enormous amounts of money on these merger / buyout transactions illegally was tremendous with prosecuted legal disputes week after week. There are issues that have possibly been the long-term effect of some businesses that could not keep up with the discipline of American businesses of the past years for long-term prosperity. Some pharmaceutical, and oil companies with a few others have maintained a level of stability, and this is productive from most everyone working for these businesses. In addition some food process company's, and farming business process disciplines have accumulated stable business operations that consist of productive, and prosperous values for the American economy, and various people of society. This means that other markets and sectors of business must restructure, and follow in their own intellectual or productive ways.

The concept of businesses, and people that are gaining a certain level of wealth that the American society can depend on for future business, and social prosperity has slightly diminished the prosperity of small and large business issues of expansion. This factor in some cases has severely diminished future issues of employee retirements which most people agree must be corrected. This may require more duties of effort from businesses, and the executive, legislative, and judicial branches of cities, towns, counties, states, and the U.S. federal government observing corporate mergers, buy-out activity, and U.S. Constitutional values of prosperity. This also will apply the right effort within providing government solutions that apply lawfully to American businesses being productive, and secured in America. Therefore the American society has to work productively to regain their true values within its diversified productive business markets, and social valued issues of society.

CHAPTER THIRTEEN
(13)

The United States Library of Congress

Markets, Legislature And The Changing Times
(13)

To observe the "markets", and the relevance of "legislative" duties in America, it is important to understand Article 1 of the U.S. Constitution as it applies to the United States legislative branch, and government. This is somewhat similar to most Constitutions of the American society of established state government disciplines. The first section (Article 1) of the U.S. Constitution "states"; that all legislative powers herein granted shall be vested in a Congress of the United States, which shall consist of a (U.S.) Senate, and a (U.S.) House of Representatives. The legal name of this legislative branch has been established as "the United States Congress".

Within the first three articles of the U.S. Constitution, it divides the powers of the United States (parallel to individual state governments) with 3 branches of government. Among the jurisdictions of the three branches of government which is: Article 1 - the legislative branch, represented by the Congress; Article 2 - the executive branch, represented by the President; and Article 3 - the judicial branch, represented by the U.S. Supreme Court. This division, with format is called the "Separation of Powers", and is therefore designed with duties to prevent any branch of government from becoming too powerful. Understanding this, the U.S. "Constitution" is a good document, but it must be amended for the changing times. This becomes the important observation, and effort for the citizens, and the American system of government including more so the Congress to make appropriate adjustments!

Considering this "Constitutional process", the American system of government has operated for more than 225 years with mostly good, occasional bad, and some evaluated Amendments to appropriate social values of logical revisions.

Throughout the American markets, and most all businesses that consist of various diversified product items, services, and sectors of business that where effected by the consolidation for various subjects of lawful legislature, certain judicial matters, and professionalism became important. This is applicable to the various state, and federal U.S. (c/o Congressional) legislative disciplines that plays an important role as the times change in the United States on almost any subject. This was evident during 1907 when the State of Missouri Attorney General Herbert Hadley, and Governor Joseph Folk filed charges against the Standard Oil (Trust) Company of Indiana (c/o Standard Oil of Ohio, Indiana & the New Jersey Company's) that consisted of over 1,400 criminal counts. Upon the filing, and ruling against the Standard Oil Company which changed the American oil industry, and laws within how they did business, this was vitally important to the vast amount of people, and companies in the oil industry throughout the United States. This established process, and ruling with the Missouri court proceedings, and how it changed one of Americas largest businesses with Anti-Trust law responsibilities also displayed how all government branches can be applied with an overall government equation. Considering this, other small oil company's where considered for equal business enforcement concerns in their regional business activities to fairly have part of these oil markets.

The courts helped change these problems within an unlawful control of oil, and gas business practices throughout America. Considering this business, and government matter was enforced with different competing gas stations located "by law" across the street from each other, but not to be associated with the "same company" gave separate opportunities. Most of these oil company enforcement issues started throughout Missouri, Indiana, Illinois, Ohio, New Jersey, Texas, California, New York, and later in other states. Within the oil industry, and society of American businesses such as the Standard Oil Company which over decades became the Atlantic Richfield Company, and more so becoming the Amoco Oil Corporation with subsidiaries, they went thru their many different changes. Within the concept of the changing times in American businesses including the oil industry, and others this vitally included state and federal legislature. These become regulated issues of the United States Congress, and the United States Department of Justice and its Anti-Trust Division including a few other departments, and agencies with important state government concerns. Their duties are to keep a logical and lawful evaluation that certain large corporations don't pursue unlawful business activities as the Standard Oil Company did before 1907.

The changing times of legislature and business markets can also be recognized in the American Automobile Industry, and even more with the massive consolidation of the telephone company's. These businesses and subsidiaries of the American Telephone & Telegraph Corporation, and now the diversified advancements of Comcast Corporation are vital example's. Observing the Ford Motor Company, the Chrysler Corporation, and the General Motors Corporation between the 1960s, and the late 1970s some businesses became engulfed with harsh competitor's with additional challenges from a vast amount of foreign automobile companies. This also included more foreign auto dealerships, and service centers with additional part manufactures like car radios, and a variety of other items. Most of these changing times consisted of a continued format of annually establishing products such as cars, trucks, and even computers from Apple Computer Corp, Dell Computer Corp., Toshiba Computer Corp, and others. Some of these computer and even telephone businesses became the wireless networking process that could be installed, or connected to most all types of vehicles with an electrical source. Comcast, AT&T and just a few others have struggled to manage this large new wireless, and mobile "service" market within logical U.S. Anti-Trust law values that even computer company's must operate from. Even with the manufacturing, and sales of accessories or parts, this legal matter increased the legislature, and established Anti-Trust divisions of government with state, and federal compliance disciplines. Now the remaining factor may be the need for computer programmers to be required to be "Licensed" due to their vicious markets, and business conflicts.

From these changing times the vital importance of the United States Anti-Trust laws were created stronger with the expansions for smaller or expanding businesses to be productively resourceful. These lawful conditions of business changes have some kind of special business opportunities of prosperity especially within those business markets that include technical and professional services to the general public. Years later this also opened up certain opportunities within markets for imported, and some exported products, and businesses. These import, and export market concerns makes the legislative issues of the advanced or changing times "Constitutionally" important from government when they must be enforced properly. This means the people have to adapt, and change with these times, and lawful resources that exist.

Considering these changing times, certain markets and U.S. legislative issues also sometimes must be considered from an international business, and American domestic format of valued social establishments within the good of U.S. foreign relations. Within the governed resources of America, these changes in society, and the government consist of values for the liability of legislative procedures. These legislative values are a balance for various U.S. Supreme Court rulings, and Constitutional Amendments to the laws that are relevant within business, and social activity. This factual concern consist of market equality for most all conditions of business liquidity, and their potential for asset prosperity values now, and in the future. Vitally this also consist of public health, and accommodation laws. These became part of the changing conditions within the establishing, and or maintaining of a well-developed American society for the people, markets, businesses, and society. In addition these lawful disciplines for most business concerns as it applies to the United States Constitution, and the laws within fair, and free markets is factually important for Americas resource of anti-competitive orders of operating standards.

The fair, and free markets of America has consisted of business products, and services that have advanced with good, and bad years for the American consumers, and even some foreign markets. America has a level of ambition to satisfy consumers in many types of markets with businesses like General Electric Corporation, United States Steel Corporation, and others that sale's products in various parts of the world just as they do in America. During the 1980s, and 1990s these businesses have had to except competitive issues from foreign company's like Mitsubishis Steel, and this becomes critical within the American system of free, and fair markets if complete management evaluations are not considered. The profit margins from a vast amount of American businesses, and corporations suffered, and this was consolidated with laying-off vast amounts of employed workers. Throughout the changing times these competitive businesses, and with certain factors of some markets that have occasionally weakened the currency rate of the U.S. dollar, this must be a subject that growing businesses need to evaluate. Just like the cost of oil and gas upon considering a vast amount of other products; the consumer then gets less "product" for the weak "dollar". Therefore, sense the 1960s, and 1970s the rate of inflation, and production cost such as within labor, and conflicting management will be a future issue to determine how American businesses, and corporations will survive long-term in the future.

Understanding the past, present, and now going into the future with the 2000 millennium, and century in America a vast amount of businesses has, and will be developing different products, and services outlined in their business procedures of discipline. One relevant important issue about American businesses and markets is that any activity they pursue must have applicable values that are consistent with the U.S. Constitution, any future U.S. Constitutional Amendments, certain U.S. Anti-Trust laws, and a variation of other laws. An appropriate example is the American Banking Industry crisis of 2008 when a vast amount of commercial banks went out of business with depositors losing money deposits that exceeded $100,000.00, and then the U.S. government (c/o the FDIC) raised the guaranteed limit on deposits to $250,000.00. Some depositors missed out, but these where business, and government activities that became challenging to the American society.

The factual activity of large corporate losses or gains is a vital observation for businesses, and markets in America to consider, but not to be overruled by destructive foreign interest, and conflicts. This is the consideration within businesses like American International Group Inc. (AIG) whom intensified American economic problems of conflict. Observing these problems in the American economy which lost enormous amounts of asset liquidity, just as foreign liquidity gained strength from the greed of Enron, and WorldCom with others a destructive junk bond market, and greed which included fraud needed to be reorganized. Contrary to those companies AGI Incorporated received a U.S. government bailout loan during 2009, and tens of billions of dollars had to be paid out to certain foreign businesses. This means more American liquidity, and currency has been paid, or relieved to foreign interest during an economic crisis in America.

These American currency assets being moved into other countries where (good & bad) investments and agreements for foreign businesses lead to wealthy individuals, and other conflicting government establishments became a weakness within the American currency. Most of these American companies had agreements with American and international investors, and business constituents that did not help the overall long-term business prosperity in America. These become the adjustments that the American people and businesses (c/o the U.S. Economy) must adapt to, and reorganize within a lawful, safe, and productive way of business. In addition this includes effective consumer decisions, manageable agreements, and with most government activities that occur a process to restructure most all conditions of the American economy. Therefore these economic formalities can be coordinated in the American society to have important business asset, and liquidity disclosers. Within the format of AIG, and other American businesses this includes most all types of detailed businesses (c/o product and service) involvements with regional or international demand, and the logical financial agreements that apply. Then these business matters should be controlled with logical American law, and legislative values of future consideration.

Considering the thousands, and or millions of changes that a vast amount of products in the United States have endured over the last 100 years, there is a condition of progress as well how these products are used at good or bad capacity rates. A certain amount of these issues may be considered difficult from the sales, and use of products like leaded and unleaded gasoline, and maybe even more so leaded paints upon how chemicals are applied to products manufactured in America. One legislative act within the Codes of Federal Regulation of determination was established to stop the manufacture, and use of lead in paint. This was factored just as they seemed to eliminate "leaded gasoline" which had similar reasoning due to environmental concerns, observing how most gasoline in now unleaded. Some of the many important concerns within American developed products of advancement is that illiterate illegal aliens whom have taken up certain job's which they can't adapt to (c/o reading and calculations) within knowledgeable decisions in a timely manner. This is the work requirement within subjects such as even color codes with certain wording for residential and more so industrial or commercial natural gas process systems including other electrical, and mechanical operating systems. As it applies to Mexicans (illegally) just like American's that can't read well (c/o colors, numbers & fractions), the American expansion of foreign language interpreted directions haven't, and don't help much in these case matters if comprehension (c/o an IQ) is low.

There is a vast amount of illegal aliens that have had a terrible and difficult time adapting to American scientific principals which includes factors of business liability. Most potentially dangerous chemical refineries, and various manufacturing facilities of certain products like the production of steel has values of caution. This steel mill level of caution and process consist of the concentration of American industry with 10,000 degree blast furnace activities that are observed as working conditions that could be potentially dangerous. Within these conditions various duties consist of the liability to control safe work requirements apart from harmful danger during production. This is the factual format of issues that within the changing times certain American companies have suffered with severe fatal accidents with advanced technology that should have been used, and operated better. Bata Steel Corporation of Indiana and a few other steel manufacturing companies is part of this problem which is keeping them from any kind of business expansion with future business operations. Just as the technology in America changes, or improves, the concept of people including employees must improve, and be prepared for the adoption of new skills. This applies to all professions, and occupations just as a vast amount of citizens in America live with the changing values of technology, and time. These technology, and timing factors are valued even more so when various people only accomplish a minimal high school education, or less which has a complex or negative effect on the American society, and business.

During the 1990s, and approaching 2008 a vast amount of American manufacturing facilities, oil and chemical refineries, and other process facilities with people have suffered from negligent explosions. With these changing or amendable conditions of industry and a lack of government enforced discipline's this problem has caused, a vast amount of American corporate small, and large businesses to consist of conflicting values of negligence. These conflicts consist of certain regional losses, and employee financial matters with additional difficulty's. Upon the social relevance this even more so includes families suffering from the loss of someone vital to the household. In a geographical consideration of these certain regions of the United States, this is where individual state government's observe industry concerns in their states natural resources, labor issues, and interstate commerce activity as it may apply to businesses. Understanding this, the state legislature is most times closely applicable to the needs of their local and regional industries.

Observation of industrial process fatal explosions and accidents can be understood as there has been coal mining issues of concern in the mountains of West Virginia, Pennsylvania, and other states far west like in Utah. These regional heavy industries of coal mining require government safety regulations applicable to new technology, and responsible change's to hopefully improve various production safety issues throughout these business disciplines in America. This is similar to the vast amount of land based oil wells in Texas, and Oklahoma upon how some consideration of off shore oil drilling, and production are considered in the future years. This vitally includes how British Petroleum Co. caused an offshore leaking oil well to contaminate the U.S. Southern Coastal waters without the best knowledge of how to clean up the oil in a preventive, productive, and timely manner. Although some methods that (BP) used, we must also observe that the U.S. government did not have an immediate solution ether for the BP Gulf Coast oil well leak. Considering government, they will outline various scientific, and industry opinions with possible enforcement concerns, but they also must be on top of their job duties as well. Therefore this means that usually as the industry, and markets throughout coal mining, oil drilling, and other processes for commodities consist of changes over the years, various business, government, and the people should observe product modifications, and changes. Considering this, the logic of local, state, and U.S. Congressional legislature becomes important with probable cause "urgently", but hopefully in a "respectfully" productive concern with advanced solutions.

The different farming within commodities of agriculture, live-stock, and food crops with other resources are important within how the farming industry changes, and then they must lawfully provide these products to the American general public. Considering this, the farmers, and their process within markets, and industry advancements, and conflicts become important to control in a geological, and agriculture format of business resources to comply, and advance with market resource capacity disciplines. The legislature is part of these factors within the farming industry that is also important to observe. This is then valued when the concentration of production, and the liability of farming has changed to the extent of how the live-stock of animals, and crops must be managed. Vitally this includes how they have considered or prepared themselves for business seasonally, and cared for this food production process.

Personal business and government inspections have relevance in these farming processes which may require public health laws, some observation of occasional other law professional concerns, and the regulatory laws of the U.S. Department of Agriculture. This American process applies to the concept of small and large farming operations that are diversified geographically. The commodities within farming have the consolidated resource values for marketing these goods within produce that are offered to a wide variety of people, and businesses. Then it is the duty of the United States Food and Drug Administration (FDA), and more so the United States Department of Agriculture (USDA) to monitor the lawful quality of these products on rare occasions in the market place. These become applicable duties to make sure safe, and responsible products are offered into different markets from most farming establishments.

Some of the changing times throughout the American farming industry has consisted of advanced farming procedures which consisted of diversified farming equipment, and the cost of maintaining a farming establishment. Farming today heavily depends on trucks, and tractors that are similar to the older days of a horse or cow, and people plowing the land within their arrangements of the harvest season, but the advanced resource of tractors is a major concept of production output. With valued agreements of logical lending form bank financing, certain tractors that are used to provide some valued, and operational duties becomes a resource of importance. These duties with various tractors, and equipment consist of some irrigation concerns, dispensing insecticides, spreading seeds, plowing soil, picking the crops (c/o some handpicked crops), and other farm duties. Contrary to these factors then all operating, and maintenance cost, including bookkeeping must be managed, even as it applies to the banking, or investments, and or investment banking. This is where managing and dependable liabilities within vehicles, equipment, and hired people have a conditional amount of time for improvements to apply farming supplies, and duties that become appropriate to their most useful capacity.

Within the farming harvest of seed, and fertilizer with routine insecticides, and irrigation these vital items have become from time to time vitally helpful to create the best yearly crop results possible. Companies like International Harvester, and John Deere Corporation sale tractors that gather hay, plow soil for planting seeds, and chopping down cornstalks which all together can have expenses, which are vital to lawful production, and their annual earnings. Contrary to this effort, this is the process that increased certain profits when farmers can have productive sales, and banking resources to work with long term financial disciplines. This also includes crop dusting with an aircraft to protect the large acres of crop land from harmful insects that will damage crops. Understanding these farming duties, and processes of harvesting food, and farming products which includes family details, the day by day accounts of these material's, and the duties within bookkeeping are vital. Therefore all the input and output financial transactions, and disciplines for most home / business farm operations are managed productively with logical equipment, and manpower including woman.

Over the last 50 to 100 years farms have become detailed with vast amounts of diversified farms, dairy farms, fruit farms, poultry farms, and the concept of truck farms. The farms taxable earnings in most markets has improved with the consistent work of growing corn, hay, oats, and soybean if no liability factors, and a lack of liquidity occur. In addition most farms are established with certain valued equipment for dairy products such as cheese, and milk from the raising of cows. The equity and liquidity within long term farming establishments depend on certain assets as part of their valued commodities. Fruit farms in North America that consist of vast amounts of trees or vines that cover large areas are considerably managed in most all logical conditions of weather. Upon the relevance of good business, this process for the many types of farmer's as businesspeople also consist of distribution.

The important process of distribution has relevance that is usually governed by regional issues of interstate commerce, and county (fair) groups within government, and social marketing events.

All markets in America have "went" thru a complex trend of supply, and demand for various products, and this effect's the American economy within the changing times. Considering agriculture products, "consumer and industrial" electrical or mechanical products, automobiles, airplanes, boats, and even houses or furniture including major appliances, the U.S. Gross Domestic Product (GDP) is an important market indicator. This is valued upon which these are diversified American products going to market at their final extent, after annual accumulated delivery. This also includes the valid observation of Gross National Product (GNP) that includes occasionally non-durable good products (basically quite similar to GDP) in America's concept of established markets with manufactured goods, and this is compared to the GNP of other countries. Management of the GDP during the 1910 to 2000 years, and decades has offered important values of taxable, and tax manageable issues (c/o deductible items) within products, and services. The legislative branch of most government concerns creates, and manages these tax rates for markets that exist in the American society of businesses, consumer purchases, and even government assets.

With most industries in America, "education" is one of Americans most valued disciplines. This becomes vital as it applies to the young, and considerably most old citizens, and professionals to understand, and keep up with. Also this vitally includes certain products, and services including conditional values within technological changes. It also applies appropriately to legislative considered amendments, and issues of "Constitutional Justice" that may change the lawful way industry must conduct certain business operating procedures. Managing these factors of education also consist of vast amounts of product and service items with supply and demand rates in America.

These many different resources within accountable business item's keeps the American system of government with small and large corporate business issues lawfully vibrant. In logical addition these international and more so U.S. domestic products are valuable as it applies to citizens, and the educated disciplines of occupations, and professions that the American society works to maintain.

Observing the massive American markets of commodities, a vast amount of environmental standards have been established to maintain the quality of air, land, and water from products that are capable of hazardous pollution for a vast amount of public health, and safety issues. Chemical refineries, and the farm land soil concerns in rural areas where strongly considered important during the early 1900s with the Insecticide Act of 1910. Approaching the years following World War II the United States Congress established the Federal Insecticide, Fungicide, and Rodenticide Act (HERA) which was to be more comprehensive thru the United States Department of Agriculture.

As industry and machinery with certain industrial processes increased, and the natural component of farming stayed nearly the same, certain issues to protect the farm soil became important. Observing the vast amount of agriculture, and farming commodities including land which certain tractors are used to work on, this farming process was occasionally in question. This was a problem "especially" due to increased machinery fuels leaking which included bad exhaust. This was also worse near some oil or chemical production facilities. Compared to the older farming duties there was slightly an argument on day by day routines to appropriate the size of the farm, and the protection of soil. Contrary to this fact these issues of farm equipment where vital, and various improvements had to be made for more effective use, and safety values that apply to most farming standards. Understanding these factors within the planting of seeds with certain contamination, and insects becoming a concern, the soil, and water environmentally had to be protected. This was in question with some illness concerns, and therefore this became the effort of an increase in government evaluations, and requirements. Also this even includes what it might mean to purchase a farm, "which on occasions" consisted of heavily contaminated soil, just like other hidden problems that would negatively affect a buyer, and any logical plans they may have.

As America's domestic product rates increased tremendously during the years of the 1950s to the 1900s the increase of environmental damages, and waste from manufactures and refineries took a toll on nature, and citizens. Due to the prosperous activity of the production of steel products, oil products, and other complex problems, the contradiction of important items manufactured or refined in the United States with government was vitally observant to establish the U.S. Environmental Protection Agency during the 1970s. The U.S. Environmental Protection Agency (EPA) then during 1970 consisted of managing the functions of 15 federal agencies dealing with the increased issue of pollution problems. The enforcement of EPA standards, and public safety research then was followed with various U.S. Congressional legislation, such as the Comprehensive Environmental Response, Compensation and Liability Act (CERCLA), and other laws to react on, and cleanup this environmental problem which improves the environmental quality in America. This format of pollution control, and environmental remediation laws was important for certain mass production industry businesses (c/o certain chemicals) to understand, and be productive with, even as it applies to vital business, and industrial restructuring.

Within additional changing times in the American society during the Richard Nixon (c/o Gerald Ford) Presidential Administrations, the Environmental Protection Agency (EPA) was created due to the many pollution compounds from residential, and more so vehicle, industrial, and commercial waste. These are hazardous and non-hazardous waste issues of pollution that where factored with larger quantities of accumulation in certain places. The levels of contamination, and pollution "before", and between the 1960s, and 1970s left Northwest Indiana with vast amounts of dead fish, and sea-life creatures on the shores of Lake Michigan. This was sustained from the heavy industrial processes of companies such as Amoco Oil Corp, U.S. Steel Corp, Inland Steel Corp, Bethlehem Steel Corp, the Lever Brothers Company, and a few others. Some issues have acknowledged that contrary to Amoco Oil (c/o BP) the U.S. Steel Corp (Gary Works Plant) and other steel manufactures where some of the worse polluter's. These companies and businesses in certain parts of the Midwest of the United States like other regions of America have endured times when supply, demand, and production becomes strong, and this appropriates an increase in industrial product output rates. Considering most individual businesses, markets, the GNP and GDP rates apart from pollution in America including the economy are considered as vitally important issues within times of prosperity. Therefore business, and this concern of future matters especially includes the future for most employed people, and must be evaluated by the businesses, and government.

During the 1980s, and 1990s more environmental groups and vast amounts of citizens took understanding of the good, and more so bad within the environmental quality of air, land, and water. Besides industry environmental remediation clean up law's, the U.S. government established the Clean Air Act, the Clean Water Act, the Oil Pollution Act, and the Safe Drinking Water Act. This was done to increase the liability effect of quality, and a safer environment from contamination. Contrary to the evaluation of new laws, and legislature in America a vast amount of corporations continued to have oil spills, certain air pollution releases, and even fatal explosions, upon which this consisted of a compounded arrangement of problems. Considering American industry standards, production, and distribution of various chemical products, most of these companies and businesses work hard to keep these problems from happening. Upon this logic they still have some work to do such as being careful with most industry critical details, and the managing of people that handle these phases of their business.

Apart from the Exxon Valdez oil spill in the Gulf of Alaska, there has been a rational amount of railroad train oil tanker cars that have spilled in excess of millions of gallons of oil including other hazardous chemicals with fumes. This has occurred in various locations throughout the United States. Besides the Texas City, Texas "British Petroleum Company" of America (formerly Amoco Oil Corp) facility, and its fatal explosion in 2005 with severe pollution to the environment, this caused a vast amount of problems. Some of these have been fatal, and environmental accidents just like a vast amount of chemical storage tank explosion's, and fire's during the present years of the 2000s. These oil tank explosions and fires caused a vast amount to high levels of overall environmental contamination with other danger to the surrounding areas. Considering at least one hundred other accidents with high levels of air, soil, and land contamination levels of danger, these conditions take a toll on the environment, and people considering accidents must be cleaned up. It also affects the businesses responsible. Therefore small and large businesses, manufactures, refineries, fuel distribution businesses, and a few others had to recognize potential problems upon which this includes any logical adjustments in the standard process of most mass production business operations.

Most businesses and markets with standard operating procedures throughout the United States was established with certain processes, and thru the years these process procedures where endured with conflict from the changing times within government, and industry. Considering the industry, and markets within healthcare over the years, and decades leading up to the 2000 millennium the American pharmaceutical companies with diseases such as leprosy, and more so the flu was found to effect a certain amount of American's as a vital problem. This health concern with the flu made certain medical concerns from the U.S. government and most American medical professionals nervous. From this health, and disease concern it then was outlined to be a vital priority, and duty to find a public health solution.

In America most diseases become an issue of importance for the public health of all citizens possible. Other diseases such as smallpox and poliomyelitis (polio) have been prevented with most all people in the United States receiving vaccinations at young ages. Within these types of medical, and government resources for American citizens, certain government values where established with pharmaceutical companies. This was done professionally so that people can live in an environment without spreading these harmful diseases that cause severe sickness to themselves, and other humans as well. Some of these same process procedures of vaccinations with slightly different problems apply to animals. These are issues that are determined by individual state legislative constituents, the United States Congress, and others in government such as the Food and Drug Administration of the United States government.

Within these continued changing times the future of American legislature will become important within health conditions including vaccines for people, and children. This is when citizens can become sick from various conditions of nature, certain products, certain business production activities, or the outbreak of a health virus that requires a vaccine. These American studies, and U.S. government scientific issues of concern with pharmaceutical vaccine efforts are to help scale down, reduce, and or eliminate the conditions of most deadly or conflicting health concerns. In addition the U.S. government health concerns have endured a serious debate within the

American citizens, and the different partisan opinions on medicine from most members of the U.S. Congress during the U.S. President Barack Obama's first administrative year.

What the President of the United States Barack Obama proposed in a healthcare bill to the U.S. Congress during 2009 is a law for all American citizens to buy healthcare insurance. My opinion is that the current system is not perfect for all people, but we must look back in years to understand, and review the U.S. government, and the health insurance industry. These conditions over the decades with business/corporate advancements to offer employee's these health benefits was a plus, but complacent government, and various businesses have allowed the economy along with health benefits to suffer devalued resources. This industry concern still has a need for quality healthcare professionals, business improvements, and a variation of good, and lawful professional, and occupational skills to keep all liabilities in order.

The concept of observing other programs or agencies within legislative issues of health care for senior citizens, and people with disabilities consist of programs that were established starting before the mid- 1940s. For "one" the Social Security Act was passed by the U.S. Congress with the valued concern of two former U.S. presidents before the 1940s which were Herbert Hoover, and Franklin D. Roosevelt which both followed the Great Depression. Second, thirty years later during 1965 both Medicare, and Medicade were added to the United States governments Social Security health care benefits plan. Then more additional Amendments to funding gave tax paying (young or old beneficiary) qualified American citizens their needed support from the Social Security Administration which was insured to their applicable eligibility! This money came from all working American citizens within their regular payroll pay check deductions by the legislative laws passed during 1976 which became the Federal Insurance Contributions Act. Understanding this payroll tax, it was established, and governed with managed duties for employees, employers, and survivors (c/o old aged citizens also) upon which certain problems consisted of people having funds when they become disable from working. This is vitally true even more so to understand the men, and woman of the U.S. Department of Defense fighting in the Persian Gulf War from 2002 thru 2010 with younger disable veterans, and their family members. These combat soldiers added to civilians of all kinds, now may have certain factors of an illness that might require the same type of medical attention, and social concerns of a vast amount of other American people.

During the years after 2002 to 2009 understanding certain parts of the future concept of American enlisted military veterans from fighting the war in Iraq, and Afghanistan the casualties, and wounded personal became a logical, and major issue. Throughout America's system of healthcare for the military and others support from the U.S. government, this has become a vital necessity to help mostly young lifetime wounded veterans. The American system of the federal government established the Veterans Administration (VA) with the U.S. Congress passing legislature such as the "Servicemen's Readjustment Act of 1944 which was followed by other benefits for veterans. The U.S. Department of Defense is a major part of this concern that has changed within certain American issues sense the Vietnam War which consisted of a high number of casualties that is similar to this time of war in the Middle East during 2009. Within this problem of military soldiers following a foreign war, occasionally long-term health problems may occur once they are discharged from service. Upon this effort in America this made the United States government observant of their obligation that provides this effort to support the families, and the veteran soldiers that have pursued these levels of war, and sacrifice. Therefore we observe a vast amount of doctors, engineers, manufacturers, pharmaceutical companies, accountants, and other professionals as vital U.S. Department of

Defense constituent members or various government contractors with expertise.

The applicable consideration of the American society has spent many years understanding the role of a vast amount of the U.S. Department of Defense contractors that are productive. Throughout the United States Defense Department, and certain government defense contractors which became an important market where the legislative branch has a logical duty of involvement, the executive branch is also a vital part. The concept of American citizens that are business owners that includes their employees on rare occasions are the people, and corporations that find themselves as committed government contractors. These are businesses that understand their markets, and most levels of the American system of government. They also have the assets to commit themselves to the product's, and service's that all levels of government in America require.

The U.S. federal financial budget, and the list of government contractors is quite long, and extensive, with amended changes, but still all budget matters must be managed in a lawful, and productive way. From the lowest form of American government to the highest branches of the U.S. federal government they purchase everything from paper, and various office supplies to cars, trucks, helicopters, airplanes, buildings, food, medicine, computers, and a vast amount of other things. This market, and U.S. government process of procurements is based on a vast amount of good, and bad events, and subjects. In 1976 the administration of the executive office of the President of the United States consisted of a cabinet of administrative offices that was numbered at 13, now during 2009 there is 21 upon which have a budget that is constantly amended. There is 435 members of the U.S. House of Representatives, and 100 members of the U.S. Senate which creates the Legislative federal branch as the U.S. Congress, and their budget is reviewed on a coordinated schedule. There is nine U.S. Supreme Court members and 11 federal circuit courts with a vast amount of federal judges, clerks, and staff attorney's (c/o public defenders) which is the establishment of the Judicial branch of the U.S. federal government. These are a few factual numbers (c/o cost items) that apply to the budget's (with specified items) that the United States government consist of within the managing duties of the American system of government.

The concept of inflation within all products and services sold as government items or services in America is a vital consideration of these government market activities. As issues are considered in the American system of government, value applies to the vital subjects such as "Health, Education, and Welfare", and others like Energy, and Labor issues with department resources. These oath driven entities of the American Constitutional format of our society is controlled by various legal disciplines from the government. This is applicable to the values within the U.S. domestic welfare, and prosperity of most all citizens. Economic values of inflation are not ignored all the time, but are discussed in state, and federal commissions, and with budget valued issues of agreements just as various federal department's apply their sectored duties. This Constitutional discipline of capacity has relevance, but the logic within studies by government strongly, and with legislature takes the price of the procurements with values under consideration. This also means that U.S. Constitutional laws, and price controls with disciplines must be applied for "appropriately", and this keeps business resource's lawfully in order.

Understanding that there is a market within government contractors, and vendors the American society including businesses has a duty along with government officials to work, and understand most procedures, and duties lawfully. Within these contractors, and vendors it also applies to each state government having "a State General Assembly" within House, and Senate members including office disciplines. This is theoretically applicable to all state and local (city & town) executive, legislative, and judicial duties, and offices.

Considering most values of doing business within government markets, these businesses are a relevant constituent of business to the American general public as well how they must hold some values of respect without discrimination or conflict. In addition, these are the efforts of American businesses that must control their lawful activity and future, just like government. Then throughout America citizens must make the best effort to be fully productive in the best interest of "citizenship values", and the land we live on in the United States of America,

INDEX